SAFETY
IN
PRESCHOOL PROGRAMS

Janice J. Beaty

Elmira College, Emerita

D1306151

PEARSON

Merrill
Prentice Hall

Upper Saddle River, New Jersey
Columbus, Ohio

Library of Congress Cataloging in Publication Data

Beaty, Janice J.
     Safety in preschool programs / Janice J. Beaty.—1st ed.
        p.   cm.
     Includes bibliographical references.
     ISBN 0-13-112040-9 (pbk.)
     1. Schools—Safety measures. 2. Education, Preschool—Curricula. I. Title.
LB2864.5.B43 2004
363.11'9371—dc21
2003044008

Vice President and Executive Publisher: Jeffery W. Johnston
Assistant Vice President and Publisher: Kevin M. Davis
Editorial Assistant: Autumn Crisp
Production Editor: Sheryl Glicker Langner
Design Coordinator: Diane C. Lorenzo
Cover Designer: Ali Mohrman
Cover photo: Corbis
Production Manager: Laura Messerly
Director of Marketing: Ann Castel Davis
Marketing Manager: Amy June
Marketing Coordinator: Tyra Poole

This book was printed and bound by R. R. Donnelley & Sons Company. The cover was printed by Phoenix Color Corp.

Photo Credits: photos courtesy of Janice J. Beaty

Pearson Education Ltd.
Pearson Education Singapore Pte. Ltd.
Pearson Education Canada, Ltd.
Pearson Education—Japan

Pearson Education Australia Pty. Limited
Pearson Education North Asia Ltd.
Pearson Educación de Mexico, S.A. de C.V.
Pearson Education Malaysia Pte. Ltd.

PEARSON
Merrill
Prentice Hall

10 9 8 7 6 5 4 3 2 1
ISBN: 0-13-112040-9

Discover the Companion Website Accompanying This Book

The Prentice Hall Companion Website: A Virtual Learning Environment

Technology is a constantly growing and changing aspect of our field that is creating a need for content and resources. To address this emerging need, Prentice Hall has developed an online learning environment for students and professors alike—Companion Websites—to support our textbooks.

In creating a Companion Website, our goal is to build on and enhance what the textbook already offers. For this reason, the content for each user-friendly website is organized by topic and provides the professor and student with a variety of meaningful resources. Common features of a Companion Website include:

For the Professor

Every Companion Website integrates **Syllabus Manager™,** an online syllabus creation and management utility.

- **Syllabus Manager™** provides you, the instructor, with an easy, step-by-step process to create and revise syllabi, with direct links into Companion Website and other online content without having to learn HTML.

- Students may logon to your syllabus during any study session. All they need to know is the web address for the Companion Website and the password you've assigned to your syllabus.

- After you have created a syllabus using **Syllabus Manager™**, students may enter the syllabus for their course section from any point in the Companion Website.

- Clicking on a date, the student is shown the list of activities for the assignment. The activities for each assignment are linked directly to actual content, saving time for students.

- Adding assignments consists of clicking on the desired due date, then filling in the details of the assignment—name of the assignment, instructions, and whether or not it is a one-time or repeating assignment.

- In addition, links to other activities can be created easily. If the activity is online, a URL can be entered in the space provided, and it will be linked automatically in the final syllabus.
- Your completed syllabus is hosted on our servers, allowing convenient updates from any computer on the Internet. Changes you make to your syllabus are immediately available to your students at their next logon.

For the Student

- **Introduction**—General information about the topic and how it will be covered in the website.
- **Web Links**—A variety of websites related to topic areas.
- **Timely Articles**—Links to online articles that enable you to become more aware of important issues in early childhood.
- **Learn by Doing**—Put concepts into action, participate in activities, examine trategies, and more.
- **Visit a School**—Visit a school's website to see concepts, theories, and strategies in action.
- **For Teachers/Practitioners**—Access information you will need to know as an educator, including information on materials, activities, and lessons.
- **Current Policies and Standards**—Find out the latest early childhood policies from the government and various organizations, and view state, federal, and curriculum standards.
- **Resources and Organizations**—Discover tools to help you plan your classroom or center and organizations to provide current information and standards for each topic.
- **Electronic Bluebook**—Paperless method of completing homework or essays assigned by a professor. Finished work can be sent to the professor via email.
- **Message Board**—Virtual bulletin board to post and respond to questions and comments from a national audience.

To take advantage of these and other resources, please visit the *Safety in Preschool Programs* Companion Website at

www.prenhall.com/beaty

CONTENTS

Chapter 1

SAFETY: THE INTERNAL CURRICULUM

STRENGTHENING THE INNER CORE
DEALING WITH FEAR

STRENGTHENING THE INNER CORE

Safety has always been an important concern in preschool programs, but never more so than today. Suddenly it seems as though the world itself is crashing down around us and our children. What can we do to keep them safe, to make them feel safe, to bring them into our programs with bright prospects and send them forth again with inner strength and a joy of life?

What Is Safety?

The dictionary defines safety as "the state of being safe from the risk of experiencing or causing injury, danger, or loss" (1999, p. 1157). But the real answer may lie in our own definition of safety and how we present it to children. What does it mean for a person to *be* safe and to *feel safe* in today's world? Some may say it has to do with protection, precaution, and prudence. Some may decide its main feature is freedom from fear. Still others who have studied the human condition say safety involves the awakening of unconditional love: that inner spiritual core of acceptance, appreciation, and compassion present in every human, but not often talked about or called upon. What do you say?

This textbook looks at safety as an internal human condition that can be developed in a specific manner, helping children become alert but not overly-fearful of dangers around them, while assisting them in becoming confident of their ability to deal with life in positive ways. This kind of safety will help both adults and children learn to draw upon strength from their own inner core of unconditional love.

Where Does Safety Begin?

Safety begins with *you*, the teacher, student teacher or teaching assistant. You must feel safe within yourself before you can help children establish their own inner strength. Safety starts on the inside. You must develop strong feelings of *acceptance*, *appreciation*, and *compassion* for yourself and others around you before you can deal with the unsafe conditions you may encounter on the outside.

How Can You Develop a Safe Feeling Within Yourself?

Self Acceptance

How do you feel about yourself? Take an honest look, a candid appraisal of your self-esteem. What kind of person do you think you are? Do you like yourself? Do you feel you are a good person, someone the children can turn to in times of stress? Or are you a worry-wart, preoccupied with every little detail that could affect you or the children in a negative manner? Are you concerned that you won't know what to do when children panic or cry? Do you yourself panic when faced with an emergency or an unfamiliar situation?

Although you must accept yourself as you are, you need to be aware of those aspects of yourself that are hard to accept, that need changing before you can help children deal with their own feelings. As you work through your feelings of inadequacy or fear, you will be able to use some of the same procedures discussed in this chapter to help children overcome their own unsafe feelings (see Figure 1.1).

Begin by writing down one aspect of yourself concerned with safety that it is hard for you to accept, that you would like to change. Do you sometimes panic when things go wrong? Write it down. Be bold about it:

SOMETIMES I PANIC WHEN THINGS GO WRONG

Look at the words you have written. Writing down feelings like this helps to diffuse their emotional impact. You are not hiding this aspect of yourself. You are admitting it—maybe for the first time. Now that you realize this is how you sometimes respond when things get out of control, you can begin to take control and change it. What else could you do when things go wrong besides panicking, or feeling fearful, or getting angry? Some people close their eyes and take several deep breaths. Others count to 10 or 20 until they regain control. There are even those who sing or hum to themselves. A few may close their eyes for a moment or two and concentrate on that spiritual core deep within them. Then they silently ask for help. Try each of these methods to see what works best for you—what brings you back to your unruffled self again. Then you can deal with whatever the situation requires calmly and quietly.

For example, try using one of these strategies when Marlon accidentally knocks over the juice pitcher and spills juice all over the table, the floor, himself, and everyone around him; or when Rhonda hits her head on the monkey bars and begins to bleed profusely; or when the fire alarm bell goes off unexpectedly for an unplanned building evacuation.

FIGURE 1.1

Strategies for Changing an Unacceptable Safety Response When Things Are Out of Control
1. Write down the response you want to change.
2. Close your eyes and take several deep breaths.
3. Count to 10 or 20.
4. Sing or hum to yourself.
5. Close your eyes and concentrate on your deep spiritual core.
6. Silently ask for help.

Self Appreciation

As you begin to analyze who you really are and what you have to offer to a classroom full of eager 3's, 4's, and 5's, you should begin to see yourself in a different light: not so nervous and unsure, but someone who doesn't fall apart under stress, who can be in control of a stressful situation. After all, you chose to work with young children like this. You chose to become a trained teacher or child caregiver. What qualities does it take to be successful in such a career? Which of these qualities do you possess? Again, write them down:

CHEERFULNESS
QUICK TO SMILE
LOVE FOR CHILDREN
PATIENCE
OPENNESS TO NEW IDEAS

Next choose one of the qualities and print it on a little sign to be mounted on the personal mirror you look in every morning to get ready for the day ahead. For instance, you might write *I SMILE A LOT*, and mount it on the mirror. Every time you see your sign it will not only remind you to smile, but also tell you what a wonderful quality you possess. Not every person around you smiles a lot, but now you can be the model. It should make you feel good about yourself as well as helping others to feel good about you. Keep up the sign for a few weeks, and then put a new sign on the mirror to help you appreciate yourself in other ways.

4

Before teachers and child caregivers can give freely of themselves to children, they need to develop a strong appreciation for their own positive qualities. When you truly appreciate yourself, you will find it much easier to appreciate others. Now you are ready to consider the third aspect of your deep spiritual core:

FIGURE 1.2

Strategies for Becoming Appreciative of Yourself as a Teacher

1. Write down positive qualities you possess as a teacher.
2. Choose one of these qualities and mount it as a sign on a personal mirror.
3. Look at the sign daily and absorb its meaning.
4. Be a model of the quality for others to see.

Teacher Compassion

Of the three aspects of the spiritual core—acceptance, appreciation, and compassion—previously mentioned, the first two apply to yourself and how you feel about yourself, your "self-esteem." But compassion involves your feelings toward others, your "other-esteem." Compassion encompasses a broad category of qualities such as: regard, respect, gentleness, kindness, tenderness, thoughtfulness, affection, and even forgiveness. It is, of course, a primary function of unconditional love.

But what has this to do with safety, you may wonder? Can feeling kindly toward a child help him to feel safe or to be safe? It can, indeed, for the feeling is unconditional. It means that you feel kindly toward a child's basic self, no matter what. He may be cross, angry, out of sorts, scared, crying, screaming, or totally withdrawn. Your positive regard for this child—if it is real—will come across to him, perhaps subconsciously. At some level he will assimilate your appraisal, which may translate itself as: If the teacher treats me kindly even when I'm screaming, then I can't be all bad. It helps him strengthen his own inner core, and he will calm down.

Whenever emergencies occur or situations get out of hand, your first response should always be to look outside yourself, to help someone else, and to apply your compassionate feelings toward others by taking action in assisting them. Can you do this? It always helps to strengthen your inner core by practicing such responses ahead of time

Once again, write down privately the name of a child you have perhaps not accepted totally, and under her name write down two or three reasons this child is hard for you to accept. For example: SHEILA—whines a lot; tattles on other children; won't play with others.

When children behave in an inappropriate manner, you realize they themselves have been treated inappropriately. Perhaps they have been too strictly controlled at home, or too harshly criticized, or never shown affection. To help yourself develop compassion toward this child, next write down two or three things you really like about Sheila. If you can't think of any, then observe her for a day or two until you discover several positive aspects, such as SHEILA: shows great curiosity; likes to paint at the easel; likes her new pair of shoes. Are you feeling better about Sheila yet? Let her know. Smile at her when you see her behaving positively. Thank her for not telling you about anyone's misdeeds today. Whisper to her how much you like her new shoes. This really works. You will change toward her, and she will change toward you and others. In addition her safety core and yours will be strengthened (see Figure 1.3).

FIGURE 1.3

Strategies for Developing Unconditional
Compassion toward Each Child
1. Write down name of child you have not accepted.
2. Write down inappropriate actions of this child.
3. Write down positive aspects of this child.
4. Show child you appreciate her positive aspects.

It may take more than a few days, of course, for changes to occur either in you or the child, but if you persist in your positive behavior toward the child, she will persist in hers toward you and everyone.

How Can You Help Develop a Safe Feeling Within Children?

Our children, our children. Consider them carefully. Our children are more than our progeny. They are our leaders and lifesavers in the world to come. And today's children are different than the children of yesterday. Ask any teacher who has worked more than a few years with preschool children and she will tell you these generations coming up are different from the others she has known. They are more sensitive, brighter, action-oriented, even hyperactive. They seem to know more intuitively without being told. A few even seem to know more than their teachers. How we treat them today relates directly to how they will treat others around them tomorrow. Although Dennis (1997) speaks to parents, her wisdom definitely applies to teachers as well:

> A young child is so impressionable that a caregiver's unfavorable or frightened response to any out-of-the-ordinary statements or activities can have untold and far-reaching consequences. It's important that parents talk to children quietly, calmly and with an open mind about what they are experiencing. (p. 175)

Child Acceptance

Concerning safety issues, once you have strengthened your own inner core, it is time to address children's feelings about being accepted, appreciated, and cared for. They need to feel safe within themselves in order not to panic when things go wrong, and in order to remain strong in the face of danger. You have accepted yourself unconditionally, now you must accept each of the children so they will feel safe in your classroom. The above exercise you performed about Sheila is the beginning of a procedure you must perform with each of the children you may not have accepted unconditionally.

Start by observing all the children unobtrusively to see what you truly feel about each of them as they work and play under normal classroom conditions. If you note some who are constantly engaged in disruption or conflict, you should consider them as children who may not yet feel accepted. Rather than responding to their inappropriate actions, try showing them you accept them (although not their behavior). When you see them doing something positive, make a note of it and let them know you approve. Do this daily until their behavior improves. As Honig and Wittmer (1996) tell us:

> The more cherished a child is, the less likely he or she is to bully others or to be rejected by other children. The more nurturing parents and caregivers are—the more positively children will relate in social interactions with teachers, caring adults, and peers and in cooperating with classroom learning goals as well. (pp. 69–70)

One teacher, who could not seem to find anything positive to say to out-of-control Jonathan, finally told him, "I like the way you breathe." It worked. After a few days he gave up his disruptive behavior and calmed down. Other activities to help children realize they are accepted include those in Figure 1.4.

Names

Children ages three, four, and five are just beginning to form a concept of who they are as a person. But even the youngest of the children understand that people identify them by their name—that is who they are. When teachers and class members call them by name, it makes them feel as though they are somebody worth acknowledging. Thus it is important for the development of a child's inner core of acceptance to hear her name spoken over and over in the class, as well as seeing her name printed on name cards, toothbrushes, blankets, and art products. Greeting children by name on a daily basis helps them to start the day feeling good. Singing their names in hello and goodbye songs reinforces that feeling. Be sure to play games with children's name cards, helping them to identify their cards by sight.

FIGURE 1.4

Strategies to Help Children Feel Accepted
1. Greet each child by name every morning.
2. Sing name songs daily being sure to include every child's name.
3. Have name place cards on meal tables.
4. Make puzzle photos of each child from photos you take.
5. Allow children to use the camera to take their own photos.
6. Take photos of children in dress-up clothes or making art or block creations to be put in scrapbooks.
7. Display children's signed art products on the wall for all to see.
8. Have children dictate a story about themselves for the scrapbook.
9. Have a private conversation with each child daily telling him or her how much you like what they are doing.
10. Read children's picture books with the theme of acceptance.

Mirrors/Cameras

Children also recognize themselves by their images. Thus a full-length mirror is a classroom necessity. Just as important is the classroom camera for use by you and the children themselves. Take many photos of each child as she completes an art or science project or as he finishes a block building or dresses up as a fire fighter. Such photos can be pasted in scrapbooks about each child, or used as a stimulus for children's dictating a story about themselves. Taking their picture is another sign that you truly accept them. But allowing them to use the camera from time to time to take their own pictures makes them feel even more important.

Self-Concept Art

Every art project can help a child feel accepted if it is signed by the child and displayed attractively for all to see. But body art activities tend to boost a child's positive self-concept more directly. Have each child lie flat on a large piece of newsprint or butcher paper and make a body tracing which can later be cut out and colored in by the child. Some teachers make body tracings at the both beginning and ending of the year so that children can see how they have grown in size and ability to color. Hand and foot stampings are another popular form of self-concept art. Children dip a hand or a foot in paint and stamp it on a white background. Children's names are printed under their own prints which are then cut out and displayed separately or left together as a large mural. Sneaker rubbings can also be made by children as they rub the side of a crayon over paper held tightly around one of their sneakers until the pattern appears.

Books with Acceptance Themes

The picture books discussed in this text can help children develop their own inner core of unconditional positive feelings toward themselves and others. The activities suggested for using each book can be a springboard into this "internal safety curriculum" you are following. The books themselves are available from trade bookstores, the publishers, or the public library. Ask children's librarians to order them if they do not already own copies.

I'm Gonna Like Me: Letting Off a Little Self-Esteem (Curtis, J. L. and Cornell, L., 2002)

Here is a humorous first-person book in rhyme by a boy in a firefighter's outfit and a girl dressed as a nurse, telling when they like themselves, even if they make a mistake. It shows them getting up, going to school on a bus, playing with friends, and being at home. They like themselves even when they eat grandma's "something new": octopus stew. (The children's favorite page.) The last page asks the reader: "How about you?" Have your small reading group tell when they like themselves. Be sure they don't start telling what they don't like!

It's Okay to Be Different (Parr, 2001)

Here is a wildly colorful book with a large cartoon character on every page humorously illustrating what it is okay to be. For example: the page telling it's okay to wear glasses shows a girl's face with huge blue glasses staring at the reader. For it's okay to have wheels, a boy in a purple wheelchair rolls briskly along. For it's okay to come from a different place, a green alien in a UFO glides through space.

Read the book to individuals or to a small group so everyone can see the comical pictures. Then encourage the listeners to make up their own "it's okay to be" about themselves. What will they say? If they start by saying silly things like: "It's okay for me to stand on my head while I eat," mention that even though this book is full of funny pictures, it is about something serious. It tells us to accept people who may be different in some way. Can they think of something different about themselves they would like people to accept? Be careful not to embarrass them.

Stand Tall, Molly Lou Melon (Lovell, 2001)

Little Molly Lou Melon is the shortest girl in first grade, has buck teeth that stick out so far you can stack pennies on them, has a voice that sounds like a bullfrog, and is often fumble fingered. But her grandmother tells her how to stand tall, walk proud, smile big, and sing out clear and strong. So she does and all the children in her new class soon ooh and aah and think she is the greatest.

After reading this book you can bring out puppets, character dolls, or people figures from the block center and introduce them one by one to the listeners. Say that each has something different it would like to overcome, and ask the children what the figure should do about it so it would be accepted. Call it your "I-Want-You-To-Like-Me Game." For instance, one puppet may be so shy it turns its head away when it talks. One block figure may accidentally knock over everything it touches. What can they do to be liked? Once the children catch on, give them the puppets and let them make up their own "I-Want-You-To-Like-Me" game. However, don't make this a game of ridicule of children's personal features that might embarrass them.

Whatever you do in reading these books to children and involving them in the book extension activities, be sure it is fun for all. Be lighthearted. The morals of the stories will become evident as you play around with the ideas and activities. From such activities and the strategies in Figure 1.4 will come a feeling of acceptance and thus worthiness for every child. As Ferber (1996) notes:

> Self-worth rests upon the experience of being loved, accepted, and cared for unconditionally. Adults can help improve children's self-esteem by giving them the message that they are fundamentally valuable in the eyes of others and worthy of care regardless of their behaviors or affects. (p. 38)

Child Appreciation

How do you show appreciation for each of the children in your class? To be accepted by you as noted above is an important first step. Next you must assess the strengths of each child: what you like about him or her; what the child has accomplished in the class; what the other children like about the child. Write down these attributes and accomplishments on a file card for each child—a Child Appreciation Card (see Figure 1.5). Each card should include positive statements such as the child's appearance, attitude, behavior, language accomplishments, physical accomplishments, cognitive development, creative accomplishments, interactions with others, and anything special or outstanding about the child. These are for-your-eyes-only cards which you may share with other staff members when appropriate, but especially to be used by you in games and activities with the children to boost their own appreciation of themselves.

FIGURE 1.5

Child Appreciation Card
Name: Donovan
Appearance:
      Wavy black hair
      Neatly dressed
      New sneakers
Attitude:
      Full of fun
      Likes other children and they like him
Behavior:
      Likes to play jokes
      Laughs a lot
      Not so noisy as earlier
Developmental accomplishments:
      Climbs to top of monkey bars
      Prints own name
      Paints lots of horses
Outstanding feature:
      Can pick up snakes without fear
      Knows the story of every book in our library

As you begin to design an activity that will help Donovan feel good about himself, you remember that when this boy first entered the class he was very noisy and almost hyperactive in his movements. He could never settle down and seldom finished anything he started. Since this card should lists only positive aspects, this is what you will be concentrating on rather than his inappropriate actions. As you focus on these positive qualities, you yourself will feel better about Donovan, and he will begin to respond more positively. Other children will also note that you are no longer so critical of Donovan's former loud and frenetic behavior, but seem to comment on more agreeable qualities.

The card itself shows how much you now appreciate Donovan. As he begins to see that you like him, the other children will note this as well, and may change their former feelings and actions toward him. Individual activities you might use with Donovan to keep him on track should focus on the likes, interests, and strengths you have indicated on the card:

Activities to help Donovan feel good about himself:
Reading the book *What Is Beautiful?* and using the mirror in the back.
Bringing in many children's books on horses.
Setting up all kinds of painting activities in art.
Putting him in charge of the classroom pet snake.
Challenging him to go hand-over-hand across the horizontal ladder.

Once you have developed a Child Appreciation Card for every child, it is possible to make up individual activities based on a child's interests and strengths. As the child becomes successful, he will realize how much he is appreciated. Because you work as a team in a preschool classroom, it is possible for one team member to take on the responsibility of observing and making out a Child Appreciation Card one at a time until the entire class is covered. The importance of such an activity cannot be stressed too strongly. As Kosnik (1993) points out:

> For children to believe that they are valuable members of the community,
> they must feel individually noticed and they must feel wanted. By getting
> to know the children and highlighting their abilities, the teacher validates
> the children. She is one step closer to increasing the children's self-esteem.
> (p. 36)

Too often teachers see their class as a *total group* of youngsters, not a collection of individual children. Children must feel *individually* noticed. Can you do it? It may be the most important action you take with the children. Will this increase their safety in the program? It will surely increase the strength of their inner core, which should in turn help them feel safe in the face of unexpected dangers.

Books with Appreciation Themes

What Is Beautiful? (Avery & Avery, 1995)

This simple book with a large painting of a person's face on the right hand page and a statement about the person in large painted letters on the left facing page, needs to be seen up close by the listener. The author Maryjean begins the book by saying she thinks David's ears are beautiful. David thinks Angela's hair is beautiful. Angela thinks Elliott's beard is beautiful. And so on throughout the book. On the last two pages a question asks the reader, "What is beautiful about you?" On the opposite page a silver paper mirror awaits a response.

After reading this book, sit in a circle with the children and ask them what they think is beautiful about the head, face, and hair of the child sitting next to them. Children enjoy this activity and can't wait till the end when they can look in the mirror and decide what is beautiful about themselves. If you don't have the book, play the game anyway, and pass a hand mirror around. Small groups are better so children do not have to wait so long for a turn.

Am I Beautiful? (Minarik, 1992)

This African animal story has Young Hippo walking across the African plains encountering various animal parents telling their babies how beautiful they are. Young Hippo shows off with dancing and twirling, but when he asks "Am I beautiful, too?" they tell him to ask someone else. When he finally asks his own mother she tells him he is the most beautiful of all because he is hers.

Listeners can re-enact this story by pretending to be each of the animals, with Young Hippo showing off in front of them. You (or they) may want to make animal ears for the characters.

Child Compassion

Compassion of any kind takes a person out of himself or herself and focuses attention on another person. In this instance, you will be helping to develop what we call a child's "other-esteem." Too often this aspect of child development is neglected both in the home and in the school. But it can actually be taught, and must be taught if we are to create a future world of caring rather than selfish people. Gilchrist (1994) who invented the term "other-esteem" has this to say about it:

> In our world today much emphasis is given to the development and enhancement of one's self-concept. We are continually reminded that we need to maintain and improve our self-motivation, self-esteem, and self-development. And yet, is there something missing from this idea of self? Perhaps we need to consider more seriously the fact that we do not live in a self-contained world. The *others* are out there and they are going to stay. So we not only have the challenge of learning about ourselves but also about other selves. Is *other-esteem* the counterpart of *self-esteem*? (pp. 1–2)

We realize that most preschool children are naturally egocentric in their behavior. They see everything from their own point of view and often believe that things happen because of them. Their preschool experience may be the first time they have had to deal with other children their age. Some youngsters become "socialized" with little difficulty. Perhaps because of previous experience with other children at home or in the neighborhood, they have no trouble taking into account the presence of peers who may want to play with the same toys as they do or to be first in every activity. They have already learned to share and take turns. But many children at first resent such "competitors" and resist giving in to their wants. In order to determine where each of your children stands in his development of other-esteem, you may want to observe and record their behavior using the Other-Esteem Checklist (see Figure 1.6).

13

FIGURE 1.6

Other-Esteem Checklist
Name:
_____Gets along with other children.
_____Can tell how another child feels.
_____Shows concern for another child in distress.
_____Allows other children to enter ongoing play.
_____Plays with others without conflict.
_____Takes turns without a fuss.
_____Shares toys and materials with other children.
_____Treats other children's materials with respect.
_____Helps another child do a task.

We as adults are often surprised that young children can tell how another child feels by looking at her, until we learn from research that even infants develop emotional cues tied to feelings. It is emotions, in fact, that guide social skills and relationships and serve as the basis for children's development of empathy and self-esteem. (Greenspan, 1997). Many preschool children can already "read faces," (i.e., tell how people feel by interpreting the emotions registered on their faces), as well as adults can. Since this is the basis for developing other-esteem, it will serve us well to provide many feelings activities, especially for those children with few check marks on their Other-Esteem Checklist.

Keep alert to emotional experiences in the classroom when someone is excited or sad or upset. Display posters of people smiling, frowning, crying, and showing anger or fear. Talk about feelings and what they look like. Play games about feelings. Make smiley-face and frowning-face masks, and ask children to guess how the wearers feel. Have children make faces in a mirror and let others guess what they are feeling. Read books about feelings and ask the listeners why they think the book character feels that way. Some feelings books include:

How Are You Peeling? Foods with Moods, (Freymann, 1999)
I Feel Happy and Sad and Angry and Glad, (Murphy, 2000)
Kinda Blue, (Grifalconi, 1993)
What Makes Me Happy? (Anholt, 1994)
Today I Feel Silly & Other Moods That Make My Day, (Curtis, 1998)
When Sophie Gets Angry—Really, Really Angry, (Bang, 1999)

In order to develop compassion for others, i. e., other-esteem, children need to be able to identify feelings. They are very good at doing this if you will give them the opportunity. Developing other-esteem is, in fact, the key to building the internal safety curriculum discussed in this chapter. Children who can identify feelings in others are less likely to panic in stressful situations. When they are able to focus on other people, they tend not to focus on themselves and their fears. As Hyson (1994) notes:

> Emotion regulation is supported in a climate where children focus on other people. Coordinating one's own desires with those of others is impossible unless one is aware of others' feelings and unless one genuinely cares about the effects one's behavior has on others. (p. 152)

Books with Compassion Themes

Truelove (Cole, 2002)

Truelove is a comical dog belonging to a couple who are having their first baby. They love their dog but have no time for him when the baby comes, so he leaves and finds love with a hilariously scurvy bunch of outcast dogs. When the couple finally find their pet and bring him home, they have to allow the whole scurvy bunch to come along with him.

If the children like this book, see if they can bring their own compassion to your "What Would You Do If?" game. What would they do if their best friend lost his favorite toy? If their pet ran away? If their best friend moved away? Have the children make up some of their own conditions.

Love Can Build a Bridge (Judd, 1999)

Naomi Judd's song "Love Can Build a Bridge" is handsomely illustrated in this book by real-looking children of different racial backgrounds responding to others in need. A girl shares her sandwich with a boy. A boy helps another boy who has hurt himself on a slide. A boy visits a girl in the hospital. A girl gives her panda toy to a boy. A girl helps a visually impaired boy walk across a fence, and so on. A cassette of the song is inserted in the back cover.

Can your children think of examples of how they have helped or shown compassion for another person? Can teams of children act out brief scenarios of compassion for the words of the song when the cassette is played?

DEALING WITH FEAR

Fear is the principal emotion preschool teachers must deal with in their efforts to keep everyone safe from harm. It is caused by the presence of something threatening or the absence of safety and security. In its lesser form fear may simply be a worry that something negative will happen. In its extreme form, however, often caused by imminent danger or the unknown, its terror may be paralyzing. Yet even lesser fears such as anxiety can produce tension of some sort: a tightening up of the body and the mind. If you are anxious you may have trouble relaxing and feeling at ease in tense situations, or in unfamiliar settings that seem threatening. (Beaty, 2002, p. 107) If you are too tense, you may not be able to take action to relieve the tension.

In young children fear seems to be age-related. It first appears in the second half of the first year when infants begin to recognize an unfamiliar face and be afraid of it. But it is not until their second year that they begin to be afraid of such things as heights, loud noises, the dark, or large animals. As they grow older and wiser children may add new fears to their makeup and drop some of the old ones. But at any age personal fear seems to be a warning signal to the human species: either reduce the threat or seek protection.

Can fear or lack of fear be inherited? Many developmental psychologists have trouble accepting the idea that any emotions are genetic. Still it is obvious that certain emotions may be absent from certain groups of people. Fear of heights, for instance, seems to be missing among many Native Americans. As adults some do well at occupations such as iron workers working on top of tall skyscrapers or bridges.

Adults and children who have developed strong inner cores of acceptance, appreciation, and compassion may not be as affected by fear as those who do not have a strong central core. Nevertheless, most people are affected in some way in situations of extreme danger. As a caregiver in a program for preschool children you need to develop a repertoire of tactics for helping children to alleviate or control their fears when emergencies occur. Strategies for Helping Children Lessen Fears, Figure 1.7, offers several suggestions with which you should become familiar.

FIGURE 1.7

Strategies for Helping Children Lessen Fears
1. Remove or reduce the cause of fear if possible.
2. Give support and comfort to child.
3. Allow child to cry.
4. Redirect child's attention to calming activities.
5. Help child to verbalize feelings.
6. Involve child in helping others.
7. Model controlled behavior yourself.

Remove or Reduce the Cause of Fear

What has caused the child to be fearful? If a particular child is responding with fear to a specific situation, it may be possible to remove or reduce the fear. For instance, when a large dog appears on the playground and one child cries, have a staff member calmly take the child inside while you shoo the dog away. If most of the children show fear of a situation you cannot control, you may be able to reduce the fear by remaining calm yourself, talking in a soft manner, and redirecting their attention by reading a story, singing a song, doing a finger play or telling a joke. For instance, when lightning flashes, thunder rumbles, and the electricity goes off, you can pull the curtains, have children sit on the floor in a Happiness Circle, and begin telling a funny story or singing a song together. Specific emergency situations are discussed in the following chapters, along with suggestions to alleviate fear.

Your safety goal for the children should be to help them gain self-control. If they are working on developing a strong inner core of acceptance, appreciation, and compassion, they may find it easy to redirect their attention away from the fear-causing situation. As more children are able to redirect attention, others will take note and follow. The situation may then turn into one of closeness, warmth, and delight in the activities you perform together.

Give Support and Comfort to the Child

Giving individual support and comfort to a fearful child may depend on your own experience in giving consolation to another. For instance, how do you help a friend who may be sobbing? Touching a shoulder, rubbing a back, putting an arm around the person or holding a hand may be your immediate response. Most children respond well to touch. In fact, neuroscientists have found that a soothing touch causes the brain to release growth hormones, while emotional stress can cause the release of the steroid cortisol, high levels of which may interfere with connections between brain cells in children. (Newberger, 1997, p. 5).

Can you hug the child or hold her close? Talk quietly as you hold her, saying that she is all right now, that it's okay to cry, and that you will stay with her until she feels better. You should repeat these words softly as long as it takes for she may not hear them at first when she is venting through tears. When the crying stops you can ask the child what she would like to do. She can continue to sit with you, but perhaps she would rather be by herself for awhile with a soft cuddly toy or a book.

A rocking chair is an important piece of furniture in every early childhood classroom for times of stress like this. Rocking a child back and forth is a calming motion for both of you. Stuffed animal toys should also be on hand for stressful situations, and the floor pillows you have in your book center can be made into a cozy nest for a disturbed youngster.

Allow Child to Cry

Young children may cry when they are afraid. But requiring children to stop crying right away is not usually the way to help them gain control of their emotions. Venting through tears is a catharsis. Studies have found that crying is of therapeutic value because the chemical toxins that are built up during stress are released in tears. In addition, blood pressure, pulse rate, and body temperature seemed to be lowered by crying. (Frey & Langseth, 1985). Psychologist Solter (1992) notes:

> Crying is not the hurt, but the process of becoming unhurt. A child who has been allowed to cry as long as needed will feel happier and more secure at school, in the long run, than a child who has been repeatedly distracted from her feelings. (p. 66)

Children need to release their distressing feelings in some manner. Some teachers try to make children stop crying because they seem to be out of control, or because the crying makes the teacher feel out of control. But it is not the tears that make children out of control. It is the stressful situation. If crying helps them to release their pent up feelings they should be allowed to cry, but at the same time you need to try to calm them down as noted. If you persist in trying to stop a child's crying before he is ready he may think you are not sympathetic. The child may stop on his own when he hears your comforting words or feels your touch.

Redirect Child's Attention with Calming Activities

Art Materials

Working with clay or play dough can help children calm down when they are in the grip of fear. Set up several tables with different art activities if the entire class is affected and let them make choices. Finger painting is another such calming activity. Children can paint on sheets of paper, directly on the table, or on the floor on rolled out butcher paper. In getting their whole bodies involved like this in swishing the paint around, they not only turn their minds away from the cause of fear, but also release energy. Movement like this in turn helps to dissipate fear through fingers, hands, and arms. Painting with brushes at easels also helps achieve the same results.

Water Play

What other creative activities can you devise for children to use fingers, hands, and arms for releasing energy like this? What about water? Vigorous water play offers the same possibilities. Have children squirt liquid soap into the water table and swish the bubbles around; or they can play with empty squirt bottles or basters in the water.

Sand Play

Emotionally distraught children also find relief at the sand table. Moving sand around with fingers and hands has the same affect as moving finger paints. Put little figures of people, animals, buildings, and vehicles in the table for children to pretend with. Some teachers keep sand trays on hand for "emergency" use for distraught individuals. Wheat (1995) notes:

> The very process of working with the sand tray regularly has helped some children immensely. Teachers have discussed how they have watched children work through sadness, anger, and disappointment and finally return to the group in a relaxed state. (p. 82)

Help Children to Verbalize Feelings

The "talking cure" also works with children as well as adults. Talk with individuals or small groups about the fear-producing situation in calming tones. When they see you are not upset they will calm down. When you offer them a chance to voice their fears they may respond with relief. Do not pressure children to talk but offer them the opportunity and then listen closely to their responses. Talking to a supportive adult helps children gain a sense of control over their feelings. In a small group situation they may come to feel better simply by hearing that other children have the same fears as they do. When they hear other children openly discussing how they feel, reticent children may find the courage to do the same. On the other hand, shy individuals may need to whisper privately to you about how they feel. You must respond positively and calmly to whatever is expressed. It takes the load off their minds for children to open up in this manner about distressing feelings.

Some teachers keep "feelings puppets" or book character dolls available for children to talk through when they are upset. They can talk to the puppets privately or have their puppet talk to your puppet. You are usually the one who must initiate such a conversation. For certain children, hiding behind a puppet is the only way they feel secure enough to express their feelings. But letting the puppet or doll talk for them gives them as much relief as if they had said the words directly.

19

Involve Children in Helping Others

One of the most effective ways of helping children to lessen their own fears is for them to help someone else. Helping another in need takes them out of themselves and their own fears. Not every child is able to do this if the fear-producing situation is too overwhelming, but some are. Let each of these children work with one other child to lessen his fear. Have them look at a book together, play with puppets, put a puzzle together, or listen to a music or book tape with headsets.

You understand that for young children, giving any kind of help to another is difficult because they first have to overcome their own anxiety caused by the stressful situation. Then they need your help in telling them what to do. You realize that in emergency situations even adults can become confused and have difficulty knowing what to do. That is the reason it is important to think through ahead of time how you will act when children begin to show fear in an emergency.

Children are also more likely to give help to others when with someone. With this in mind you might decide to ask two children to help a third youngster by playing with materials together. You will be distracting all three children from the fear situation in addition to helping them strengthen their inner core of compassion.

Model Controlled Behavior Yourself

You are the one the children will look to in times of stress. How do you handle yourself? Even if you feel upset and are on the verge of panic you must pull yourself together in front of the children. Later you can let out your feelings if you still need to. Figure 1.1, *Strategies for Changing an Unacceptable Safety Response When Things Are Out of Control* may give you several suggestions on how to alter an inappropriate response.

Realizing you must model controlled behavior in front of the children can actually help by taking you out of yourself and your feelings just as it does for children who help others in times of stress. Children will be looking at you to see how they should respond to the stressful situation. You must look unruffled, talk calmly, and behave in a composed manner. Smile at the children. Mention how good it is to see everyone behaving normally. You might sing a soothing song together. Help them to carry on as they ordinarily would. You will be practicing other-esteem in a real and important way. Now may be the time to read a book with an overcoming fear theme.

Storm in the Night (Stolz, 1988)

Young Thomas and his cat Ringo are living with Thomas's grandfather the night the thunder storm strikes. When the electricity goes out and the TV goes off there is nothing to do but tell stories. Grandfather takes Thomas out on the porch and tells him a tale about a storm as scary as the one they are experiencing. As lightning flashes and thunder crashes he relives the fearful experience when he was a boy, in which he was too frightened to go outside and rescue his new little puppy. But as he thought about his puppy he forgot about his fear, and was finally never again afraid of storms.

Because it is a longer story than most preschool children are used to, you may need to "read" the pictures—wonderfully dark, realistic portrayals of the old man, the boy, and the cat in the blue-black of night. Read to individuals or a small group so that everyone can see the outstanding illustrations. Afterwards ask the children what they would have done in the same situation. Would they have gone out on the porch? Would they have rescued the puppy? What gave Thomas the courage to sit outside in the storm?

Earthquack! (Palatini, 2002)

In this comical take-off of Henny Penny's "the sky is falling" nursery tale, Chucky Ducky hears the ground grumble, feels the ground rumble, and then with a stumble falls down in a tumble. He thinks it is an earthquake and rushes to tell his barnyard friends one by one: Lucy Goosey, Vickie, Nickie and Rickie Chickie, Brewster Rooster, and on and on, who each in turn pass the word along. In the end it turns out to be only Joel and Lowell Mole digging a tunnel on their way to San Jose.

It is a cumulative tale full of silly sentences and rhyming words which should capture the attention of all the youngsters as they laugh over the whimsical pictures of the alarmed animals. But the underlying message is a safety reminder of what turmoil can result from an unfounded rumor. The children can re-enact the story with different ones playing animal parts and everyone stumbling and tumbling as you read the words.

THE CHAPTERS TO FOLLOW

The chapters to come treat safety in preschool programs from a teacher's point of view. *Chapter 2, Safety: The Indoor Curriculum* discusses how the physical layout of the building and the classroom can be set up with safety in mind. Each classroom learning center is shown promoting safety by the way it is set up, the toys and materials available, and the safety activities that can result. The building layout with its stairs, doors, halls, entrances, and exits is also visualized from a safety perspective. Bathrooms are also shown as high in priority for safe usage by children and classroom staff.

In *Chapter 3, Safety: The Outdoor Curriculum* it is the building, grounds, and parking space that are first discussed. But it is how the playground with its layout, fencing, surfacing, and array of play equipment addresses safety that is featured. In addition, street safety, transportation safety, and field trips are discussed.

Chapter 4, Emergency Preparedness takes on more significance than ever in our unpredictable world. How teachers deal with children's accidents, illnesses, and injuries requires knowledge of injury prevention and first aid procedures. Emergencies discussed include catastrophic events, accidents, fire emergencies, weather emergencies, and natural disasters. Carrying out drills and evacuations are demonstrated.

Chapter 5, Personal Safety describes a therapeutic approach to child emotional abuse, physical abuse, sexual abuse, and neglect, stressing prevention, detection, and intervention (healing).

Chapter 6, Teaching and Learning Safe Behavior discusses the role of self-directed play in children's learning about safety. Safety concepts are learned through the use of small toy prop boxes in learning centers, dramatic play with costumes and hats, with puppets and book character dolls, and through teacher-led follow-the-leader games.

THIS CHAPTER'S ROLE

Before teachers can deal with the details of the safety curriculum to follow they must have centered themselves internally and opened up to acceptance, appreciation, and compassion for themselves and their children. Then they will be able to deal with the fear that accompanies so many safety situations. As Montagu (1995) reminds us:

> A teacher of young children, more than anything else, must be able to love children unconditionally, to be able to communicate to them, without any patronizing and without any strings attached, that she is their friend—for friendship, it must be understood, is just another word for love. (pp. 42–44)

WHAT HAVE YOU LEARNED FROM THIS CHAPTER?

1. How is unconditional love connected with safety?

2. How does compassion toward another person apply to safety?

3. When emergencies occur what should be your first response?

4. How are many of today's young children different from yesterday's?

5. Why is it important for you to use a child's name frequently?

6. In what ways can you show appreciation for individual children?

7. What is "other-esteem" and how will you know if a child possesses it?

8. How does the fear emotion develop in young children and how can you help them control it in stressful situations?

9. Why should you allow a child to cry when she is afraid?

10. How can verbalizing feelings help children overcome fear, and how can you help a child talk about his feelings?

HOW CAN YOU APPLY WHAT YOU HAVE LEARNED?

1. Write down one of the unacceptable safety responses you possess that you would like to change and go about changing it. What did you do and what happened?

2. Write down the name of a child you have not accepted unconditionally and tell how you will go about changing your feelings. What happens when you do this?

3. Describe in detail two activities involving a child's name and tell what happens when you carry them out.

4. Describe and carry out a self-concept art project. How do the children respond?

5. Read a book with an acceptance or appreciation theme. Talk to the children about the story afterwards and describe their responses.

6. Carry out an activity that helps children identify their feelings and tell how they respond.

7. Set up a calming art activity and help a child become involved during a tense situation. Tell what happens.

8. Help a child assist another child who exhibits fear and tell what happens.

9. Model controlled behavior yourself during a stressful situation, telling what you do and how children respond.

10. Read a book with an overcoming fear theme and have the children re-enact the story. How can you tell if they understood the concept?

REFERENCES

Beaty, J. J. (2002). *Observing development of the young child.* Upper Saddle River, NJ: Merrill/Prentice Hall.

Dennis, C. *The millennium children.* (1997). Clearwater, FL: Rainbows Unlimited.

Ferber, J. (1996). A look in the mirror: Self-concept in preschool children. In L. Koplow (Ed.), *Unsmiling faces: How preschools can heal.* New York: Teachers College Press.

Frey, W. H., & Langseth, M. (1985). *Crying: The mystery of tears.* Minneapolis: Winston

Gilchrist, A. (1994) *Conflict and other esteem: The counterpart of self-esteem.* Unpublished manuscript. Columbia, MO: Central Missouri Foster Grandparents Program.

Honig, A. S., & Witmer, D. C. (1996). Helping children become more prosocial: Ideas for classrooms, families, schools, and communities. *Young Children, 51*(2), 62–75.

Hyson, M. C. (1994). *The emotional development of young children: Building an emotion-centered curriculum.* New York: Teachers College Press.

Kosnik, C. (1993). Everyone is a V.I.P. in this class. *Young Children, 49*(1), 32–36.

Montagu, A. (1995). Friendship—loving: What early childhood education is all about. *Child Care Information Exchange.* 106, 42–44.

Newberger, J. J. (1997). New brain development research: A wonderful window of opportunity to build public support for early childhood education. *Young Children, 52*(4), 4–9.

Random House Webster's College Dictionary. (1999). New York: Random House.

Solter, A. (1992). Understanding tears and tantrums. *Young Children, 47*(4), 64–68.

Wheat, R. (1995). Help children work through emotional difficulties: Sand trays are great! *Young Children, 51*(1), 82–83.

SUGGESTED READINGS

Beaty, J. J. (1999). *Prosocial guidance for the preschool child.* Upper Saddle River, NJ: Merrill/Prentice Hall.

Deskin, G., & Steckler, G. (1996). *When nothing makes sense: Disaster, crisis, and their effects on children.* Minneapolis, MN: Fairview.

Greenman, J. (2001). *What happened to the world? Helping children cope in turbulent times.* New York: Bright Horizons Family Solutions.

Gross, T., & Clemens, S. G. (2002). Painting a tragedy: Young children process the events of September 11. *Young Children, 57*(3), 44–51.

National Association for the Education of Young Children. (2001). Helping young children in frightening times. *Young Children, 56*(6), 6–7.

Oehlberg, B. (1996). *Making it better: Activities for children living in a stressful world.* St. Paul, MN: Redleaf Press.

CHILDREN'S BOOKS

Anholt, C., & Anholt, L. (1994). *What makes me happy?* Cambridge, MA: Candelwick.

Avery, M. W., & Avery, D. M. (1995). *What is beautiful?* Berkeley, CA: Tricycle Press

Bang, M. (1999). *When Sophie gets angry—really, really angry.* New York: The Blue Sky Press.

Cole, B. (2001). *Truelove.* New York: Dial.

Curtis, J. L. (1998). *Today I feel silly & other moods that make my day.* New York: Joanna Cotler Books.

Curtis, J. L., & Cornell, L. (2002). *I'm gonna like me: Letting off a little self-esteem.* New York: Joanna Cotler Books.

Freymann, S., & Elffers, J. (1999). *How are you peeling? Foods with moods.* New York: Arthur A. Levine Books.

Grifalconi, A. (1993). *Kinda blue.* Boston, Little, Brown.

Judd, N. (1999). *Love can build a bridge.* New York: HarperCollins.

Lovell, P. (2001). *Stand tall, Molly Lou Melon.* New York: G. P. Putnam's.

Minarik, E. H. (1992). *Am I beautiful?* New York: Greenwillow.

Murphy, M. (2000). *I feel happy and sad and angry and glad.* New York: Dorling Kindersley.

Palatini, M. (2002). *Earthquack.* New York: Simon & Schuster.

Parr, T. (2001). *It's okay to be different.* Boston: Little, Brown.

Stolz, M. (1988). *Storm in the night.* New York: HarperCollins.

Chapter 2

SAFETY: THE INDOOR CURRICULUM

CLASSROOM SAFETY
BATHROOM SAFETY
ENTRANCES AND EXITS

CLASSROOM SAFETY

Children in Learning Centers

What do you see when you enter an early childhood classroom in action? Children, children everywhere: dressing up in grownup clothes, building towers of blocks, pounding nails in tree stumps, swishing paint across easel paper, curled up with books on beanbag chairs, or climbing a ladder to a loft. They are here, there, and everywhere. But before you can blink the scene has changed, and the children have switched to different activities in other areas of the classroom. They are following their interests or trailing their friends to one after another of the exciting classroom learning centers.

How safely these activity areas are used depends upon how you as a teacher have set them up. Are water tables filled to the brim? Then expect slippery floors from spilled water to send unwary youngsters sprawling. Are high shelves stuffed with enticing materials? Then expect boxes to come tumbling down on heads when little hands reach high above their heads. Are safety goggles missing from sand tables? Then expect tears and complaining when sandy fingers rub unprotected eyes. Is the dress-up area too small for all who want to use it? Then expect pushing and shoving and lots of loud protesting. Fye and Mumpower (2001) remind us:

> A warm, nurturing, stimulating environment tells children that they are valued and that they, and their ways of learning, are understood and respected... Safety and accessibility are also essential when designing any learning environment. Make sure that all equipment and furniture are suitable and safe for young children. Furniture is arranged to enable children, including those who use mobility aids such as wheelchairs or braces, to move about freely. (p. 16)

Setting Up Learning Centers with Safety in Mind

When teachers initially set up their classrooms, their principal concern is often children's learning rather than their safety. Although we give lip service to "safety first," we tend to consider safety afterwards. This text wants to serve as your reminder that safety should be considered neither first nor last but *at all times*. Safety can be built into every classroom learning center if teachers keep in mind that each component of the program should support children's physical, mental, social, and emotional well-being.

Learning centers themselves are the principal means for articulating the program's curriculum: showing children what materials and activities are available for them to use and challenging them to use them appropriately. The safety elements these centers can address include the number of children in each center, the kinds of toys and materials in use, how they are set up to encourage children's independent use, and whether water or electricity are necessary ingredients in a particular center.

A simple method some teachers use to arrange their classroom space is by dividing the room into four separate sections as suggested by Lay-Dopyera and Dopyera (1990): quiet and dry activities, quiet and wet activities, noisy and dry activities, and noisy and wet activities. By grouping appropriate learning centers together in each of the four sections, children are able to function safely and more effectively. For instance, in the quiet and dry section, teachers can set up the book center, writing center, computer center, and manipulative center.

Quiet and Dry Activities

Book Center

The book or library center needs to be one of the most inviting learning areas of the classroom in order to invite children to curl up with an enticing book. It can be a cozy nook in a corner of the room, or even a bay window with plenty of floor pillows. Comfort and safety can team up if appropriate carpeting keeps the center warm in cold weather but inviting for children to sprawl on the floor with a book any time. Be sure that floor pillows or beanbag chairs do not cover heat vents accidentally. An adult rocking chair at one side invites staff members to read to children on their lap while taking care not to rock on fingers of children lounging nearby on the floor. You may need to help children learn to control child-size rockers so they don't get carried away with their rocking and tip over or rock on someone's fingers. Keep bookshelves low enough so children will not be tempted to climb up for out-of-reach books.

The size of the area depends on whether it will be used by teachers for reading to small groups or only by individual children during free choice periods. Many teachers help children to regulate their own numbers in the centers by posting a sign at the entrance to each with a numeral or stick figures showing how many children may use the center. Some provide center necklaces: one for each child allowed.

Writing Center

In many classrooms the writing center consists of a table with child-size chairs around it and a shelf with writing materials nearby. Because this is such an important learning center these days for promoting emergent literacy, teachers should use their imaginations to design a more inviting area children will be drawn to and use independently. What about an office? Desks, desk lamps, bulletin board, file cabinet, manual typewriter, pencil sharpener, play telephones or cell phones, a calendar, and writing supplies make it seem real to children. Pens, pencils, markers, pads and tablets, envelopes, stationery, typing paper, stamps and stampers, paper clips, and paper punchers can be stored on shelves or in the pigeonholes or drawers of a desk. A roll-top desk is an exciting piece of furniture for children to use. Fye and Mumpower (2001) have this to say about furniture:

> Child-sized furniture and safety are primary factors in the selection of pieces, all of which should meet current safety standards. Comfort and convenience are necessary because furniture in early childhood classrooms is expected to be moved often and may have many different uses. (p. 18)

For safety's sake, place the desks against the wall with the wires from lamps plugged into a socket directly behind the desk and without extension cords. Any wall sockets not in use should be childproofed with covers. Encourage children to use materials only in the center. Pencils with sharp points, for instance, can accidentally stab someone when carried in a child's swinging hand outside the center. The number of children can be regulated by the number of desks and chairs available, as well as a number sign or necklaces at the entrance. Have the typewriter on a separate table or desk. More than one child may want to use it at once as they experiment with the keys. A computer and printer can also be included in this center if there is room, or set up as a separate center.

Computer Center

Set up this center for two seated children to use the computer at a time. Three to five-year-old youngsters can teach one another as they teach themselves how this powerful interactive tool works. Keep the keyboard and monitor as close together as possible so children begin to understand cause and effect as they press one key at a time. The monitor screen should be at the children's eye level when they are seated, not on a shelf above them. Most computer desks are made for adults and not really suitable for children who tend to stand at them when they should be sitting in front of the keyboard and monitor. Place the printer on the same table or desk. Electric cords should be plugged into a surge protector bar under the table or a wall outlet behind the machine and out of children's reach. Do not use extension cords that children can trip over. To prevent damaging spills, cups of water or other liquids should never be placed on the computer table. Have children wash their hands before use to prevent sticky fingers from gumming up the keys. When not in use cover the keyboard or move it out of reach to prevent children from playing with the keys or inserting tiny objects.

Manipulative/Math Center

Counting, sorting, and math activities should be included in the manipulative center for preschoolers to experiment with. If you have three-year-olds or younger children in the programs, but sure the counters and stringing beads are too large to be stuffed up little noses or into ears. Use large counting and sorting items whenever possible, keeping them stored in marked plastic containers when not in use. Materials should include puzzles, table blocks, sorting and matching games, shape, color, counting and number games, toy cash registers, an abacus, weighing and measuring devices, and number beads or rods. Check games and toys for broken or missing parts and discard anything with splinters, wires, or peeling paint. Change materials from time to time to add variety, but be sure to include enough of the favorite materials to prevent squabbles. A table or floor with flat carpeting and nearby shelves should serve four to six children at a time.

Quiet and Wet Activities

Art Center

Art activities should be located near a sink for easy use of water and cleanup. Equipment should include easels placed side by side for socializing by the children as they paint, tables for flat painting and crafts, and open shelves for storing paper, paints, brushes, crayons, scissors, dough, yarn, fabrics, and other collage materials. Teachers' art supplies should be stored in cabinets inaccessible to children.

Surprising as it may seem, children's sharp scissors are less dangerous for youngsters to use than dull ones. Scissors should be easy, not difficult to use, or children who are trying too hard may slip and cut themselves. Be sure to provide left-handed scissors for those who need them. Teachers should keep a watchful eye on all children when scissors are out, and have them put the scissors away in holders on nearby shelves when not in use. They should not be taken out of the center by children.

All art materials for young children should be nontoxic, nonflammable, and water based. (Taylor, 2002) Remove or replace all hazardous art materials such as rubber cement, which is toxic if inhaled. Use white glue instead. Have children wear safety goggles when using modeling sand to prevent them from wiping their eyes with sandy fingers. When using glitter, have children apply it from a shaker and keep fingers away since glitter can also be dangerous to eyes. If glitter gets on hands or fingers, children need to wash it off before it is rubbed in their eyes. Do not use tiny craft and collage beads, buttons, and gems that the youngest children may put in their mouths, noses, or ears. Remember also that water spills need to be cleaned up immediately to prevent falls on slippery floors. Children can help. Not only do they enjoy such grown-up tasks but they also discover the safety reason for quick cleanups if you make the point. Because such spills are likely, washable floor coverings are most practical.

Science/Discovery Center

Science centers are often located on a table or counter along the wall or under a window where sunlight for plant experiments is available. The tools of science such as magnifying glasses, magnets, binoculars, children's microscopes, collecting nets, jars, and bottles can be arranged for use on open shelves. On the other hand, children's collections of seeds or beans should be displayed under clear plastic wrap instead of leaving them open for handling. Some children tend to put such items in their mouths, and certain seeds or beans may be poisonous.

House plants, too, can be highly poisonous if ingested, and thus pose a problem for children who may be tempted to eat a leaf or berry. Keep all live plants out of reach. Rather than warning children against eating such leaves or berries, it is safer to remove the temptation. If you stress "no eating," certain youngsters are sure to try it just because you mentioned not doing it. Figure 2.1 lists some of the common poisonous and safe plants. (American Academy of Pediatrics, 2002, p. 434)

FIGURE 2.1

POISONOUS INDOOR PLANTS
Philodendron
Mistletoe berries
Dieffenbachia
Poinsettia leaves
Amaryllis

POISONOUS OUTDOOR PLANTS

Holly berries	Yew
Mustard	Lilly-of-the-valley
Hydrangea	Mushroom
Buttercup	Bittersweet leaves
Azalea	Black locust tree
Castor beans	Rhubarb leaves
Rhododendron	Cherry tree
Datura	Oleander

SAFE INDOOR PLANTS

African violet	Impatiens
Begonia	Jade plant
Boston fern	Rubber plant
Christmas cactus	Swedish ivy
Hen-and-chickens	Yellow day lily

If a child should ingest a poisonous plant, immediately call the Poison Control Center whose number should be placed on the wall next to a phone. Follow their directions before treating the child.

The science/discovery center is usually the location for the classroom aquarium, incubator, pet cages, or perhaps an ant farm. Children will be taking turns feeding the fish and feeding and watering the pets on a daily basis. Watch out for food and water spills and help children clean them up before someone slips and falls. Pets may include gerbils, guinea pigs, mice, and even a snake. Teachers should be responsible for cleaning pet cages on a daily basis before the children arrive. Talk to individuals and small groups about the careful, gentle handling of the animals if this is permitted, and be sure a staff member supervises. Planting seeds in pots, cups of dirt or trays by children should also be supervised to prevent seeds from being spilled or put in mouths or noses.

Noisy and Dry Activities

Block Center

Blocks and their accessories should take up more space in the room than most other activities. Several shelves, both against the wall and also sectioning off the center from other areas should hold a large selection of unit blocks and hollow blocks, along with the small trucks, cars, figures of people, doll house furniture and other props free of broken parts for use with the blocks. The free-standing shelves should be low and sturdy enough not to tip over on children when in use. Flat carpeting makes an ideal floor space for building. Keep it roomy enough for a number of children to build large buildings. Riding trucks do not belong in the block center where they may crash into buildings or the builders. Likewise table blocks and their tables should be located in the manipulative area.

The principal safety concern in the block center is the height of the buildings. Some teachers allow children to climb on chairs to build high towers. Others permit children to build only as high as a child's own height while standing on the floor. The danger is twofold: tall buildings may fall on another child, and climbing children may themselves fall and be injured. You must decide on your own safety priorities, and then establish block-building rules with the children at the outset. As with other learning center rules, make them simple and use illustrations for these pre-literate children to understand. For instance, you can draw an outline of a block building next to the outline of a child to show the allowable height of a building, and another showing a building that is too tall. Write the simple rules under each: "just right" and "too tall."

Dramatic Play Center

Another large center is the dramatic play area where dress-up clothes and child-size furnishings for kitchen, store, or office are located. Toy safety is the principal concern in this center. Check the dolls for parts that a child could twist off and swallow accidentally. Remove any dolls with buttons, glass eyes, and beads that are sewed or wired on. What about the jewelry children may use when they dress up? Earrings should be large and strings of beads unbroken. Remove any toys with springs, wires, or sharp parts.

Also check the cupboards and drawers for any broken or cracked plastic ware. Be sure plastic dishes, knives, and spoons are not broken. Where are the dress-up clothes kept? Most teachers prefer to have them hanging from hooks in this center for easy selection and return, rather than stuffed in drawers or boxes. Be sure the hooks are not at the children's eye level. Higher, but still within reach, is better. If you are using throw rugs in this center, be sure they have a non-skid backing to prevent falls.

After field trips to fire stations, doctors' clinics, or construction sites this center may be set up with special props to help children play the roles they saw enacted in real life. For instance, a repairman's role may require the use of tools such as toy or real screwdrivers, wrenches, pliers, wires, screws, bolts, and fuses. Teach children their proper use and supervise them closely. When not in use, keep such props in plastic tool bags or a fishing tackle box. (Isbell, 1995, p. 45) Other centers you may set up after a field trip include bakery, fast food restaurant, gas station, supermarket, museum, or hospital. Be sure to check any props you provide for their safety features. Try to visualize how children will use, and especially misuse, these props to see if they embody anything dangerous.

Large Motor Center

Most early childhood programs with room enough try to provide an indoor area for exercising children's large muscles in jumping, climbing, crawling, sliding, or throwing and catching. It may include an indoor climber, a loft, large plastic snap blocks for building structures to be climbed on or crawled through, a child's basketball hoop, a balance beam, and bean bag or ring toss game. It may be located in the classroom, or in a separate room or gymnasium. Safety features need to include thick cushioning under indoor climbing equipment and safety rules for using wheeled riding vehicles and throwing balls. A loft within a classroom provides an excellent opportunity for climbing up a ladder and sometimes sliding down a slide. Fye and Mumpower (2001) point out:

> A loft with a removable ladder makes it possible for an adult to control access
> to the area. Lofts should be monitored at all times and the number of children
> playing in them limited. (p. 22)

Choose equipment carefully with safety in mind. For instance, most teeter-totters are too difficult for preschoolers to use without injury. Lofts should not be higher than an adult's eye-level. Be sure any railing around the loft has slats spaced close enough that children's heads cannot be entrapped. Indoor balls should be soft such as inflated beach ball types or made of yarn or sponge-like material. It is not necessary for them to bounce on the floor within the classroom or they may hit someone accidentally. Use them for throwing and catching practice. Even children in wheelchairs can throw and catch soft balls. Use your ingenuity to accommodate everyone in all activities while keeping safety in mind.

Music/Listening Center

The music center is sometimes a small space where music equipment is kept which can be used by the total group in a larger area. A pegboard for hanging rhythm instruments will be on the wall. Shelf space can accommodate drums, xylophones, and larger instruments. On the other hand, the music center can also be a listening center for making, listening to, and recording all sorts of musical rhythms, beats, songs or children's stories. In this case it may include a record player, a tape recorder and player, a jackbox with headsets, and perhaps an electronic keyboard. It may also include a little 9-inch TV-VCR for showing safety videos to small groups. Children can be taught how to use the equipment safely and independently.

Electric cords for any of these players should be out of children's reach, and they should not be allowed to plug or unplug the equipment. Battery-powered players are safer for young children to use. But avoid equipment with small mercury-type batteries that could be swallowed accidentally. If youngsters use headsets for listening, be sure to control the volume on the player in a permanent manner to prevent loud sounds from damaging children's hearing.

Woodworking Center

Some teachers do not include a woodworking center because of the safety problems it entails—or perhaps because they are uncomfortable with woodworking themselves. This need not be the case if the center is set up carefully for a limited number of children at a time, say two by providing two pairs of safety goggles. Both girls and boys enjoy working with hammers, nails, and wood, and can easily learn to work safely with tools. A small adult hammer works better for young children than toy set hammers for driving nails into wood. Pounding nails has proved to be one of the best activities for promoting children's eye-hand coordination, as well as for working off frustration in a harmless manner.

It is not necessary to have a full-fledged woodworking center with a workbench and shelves full of tools. Instead, start with two sawed off tree stumps and have children pound nails into the top. Thick carpeting or rug squares under the stumps cuts down on noise. Have children wear safety goggles (they love to!), and have a staff member or parent demonstrate to one child at a time how to hold the hammer and pound. When the stump top is covered with nails, saw off a two-inch slice, and start again. Children can help make rules for the center, including: "two children at a time;" "wear goggles at all times;" "use saw, hammer, or drill only when adult is present." Children with weak muscle tone can hammer independently if you add golf tees and Styrofoam to the center. (Flynn and Kief, 2002, p. 21)

Noisy and Wet Activities

Water/Sand/Sensory Table

Here is another learning center where goggles are essential whether water, sand, or another material such as rice, oatmeal or dirt is in the table. The number of goggles you provide tells children how many can play there at a time. Keep water, sand, or other materials low in the table to prevent spills and falls. Rice spilled on the floor is even more slippery than water. Clean it up immediately. Keep a child-size broom, mop, and dustpan in the area for children to help. Toys to be used in the table can be kept on low shelves nearby. Be sure they are not broken, sharp-edged, rusty, or made of glass. In water use plastic cups, bottles, funnels, droppers, and basters instead. Do not use straws. Although children enjoy blowing bubbles in the water through straws, they too often suck up and swallow the water as well, which may contain germs.

When water is to be used in the table, clean and sanitize the table first with a bleach solution. Also clean and sanitize the toys to be used. Avoid using sponge toys which can harbor bacteria. Discard the water when water play is over. Do not use the same water with different groups of children or at different times. (Stoll, 2000, p. 104)

Cooking Center

Most cooking centers are temporary areas where a teacher and small group of children may prepare a snack or a special food. Such centers are not open to children's independent use during the free choice period. You as teacher need to know the state, local, and school insurance and safety regulations governing hot food preparation. Some schools do not allow electric appliances such as microwave ovens, toaster ovens, hot plates, or blenders in the classroom. Some require special kitchen areas for hot cooking.

An adult should always be in the area during food preparation. Young children can learn to use paring knives and scrapers safely, but an adult should supervise. Have a child start by cutting cooked vegetables or soft fruits such as bananas with a plastic knife. Then they can try using a sharp knife. If permitted, electrical equipment can be plugged into counter-top outlets which are otherwise covered when not in use. For instance, a cake can be prepared in the classroom, but then taken into the kitchen for baking.

Child's Private Area

Children in a group setting need a safe and comfortable private area to retreat to at various times during the day. An overstuffed chair, a card table covered with a blanket, on top of or underneath a loft, or a large cardboard box with a door cut in it and floor pillows inside make excellent private spaces. Many children need to pull away for awhile from turbulent group activities, to "take a breather" while they rest or collect themselves. When they return to the group refreshed, they are more likely to work or play in harmony and less likely to cause an accident or a disruption. Bunnett and Davis (1997) report:

> We discovered that children need more than one "cozy nest," and designed several soft and quiet places. Over the years we have used mattresses, bean chairs, hammocks, and rag pillows, to name a few. We found that with additional spaces children can do their work with fewer disruptions, feel less fatigued, and can retreat to a quiet place without negative connotations. (p. 44)

How Can You Keep Learning Centers Safe?

Once the learning centers are set up with safety in mind, you are on your way. But since safety is an ongoing practice, you must also check the premises for safety on a daily basis. The most effective and least intrusive method involves using a simple checklist made for your own program like the one in Figure 2.2, which was made for the centers described in this chapter. Run off several copies and go through them daily as you prepare the centers for the children every morning. Then make the necessary safety adjustments.

FIGURE 2.2

Learning Center Safety Checklist

Book Center
_____Appropriate carpeting
_____Heat vents not accidentally covered
_____Rocking chairs away from children on floor
_____Bookshelves low and sturdy

Computer Center
_____Monitor on child-size desk at eye level
_____Electric cords in surge protector bar out of children's reach
_____Water or liquids kept out of center

Art Center
_____Scissors use supervised
_____Toxic materials (sprays, solvents, glue) removed
_____Water spills cleaned up
_____Goggles used with modeling sand, glitter

Block Center
_____Free-standing shelves low and sturdy
_____Building heights within limits
_____Block accessories free of broken parts
_____Riding trucks kept out of center

Large Motor Center
_____Climbing, balancing equipment cushioned
_____Safety rules for riding vehicles
_____Loft at adult eye level; railing slats close together
_____Balls made of soft materials

Woodworking Center
_____Small adult-size tools supervised
_____Safety goggles used
_____Safety rules established and enforced

Cooking Center
_____Cooking appliances in compliance with safety codes
_____Sharp implement use supervised by adult
_____Electric appliances, microwave ovens controlled by adult

Writing Center
_____Desks against wall
_____Lamps plugged into wall sockets
_____No extension cords
_____Sharp pencils kept in center

Manipulative/Math Center
_____Tiny beads or counters removed
_____Materials with broken parts, peeling paint discarded
_____Sharp or pointed objects eliminated

Science/Discovery Center
_____Children's collections covered with clear plastic wrap
_____Aquarium, incubator wires out of reach
_____Houseplants nonpoisonous
_____Pets handled gently; cages clean

Dramatic Play Center
_____Dolls, toys with no small removable parts
_____Earrings large; strings of beads unbroken
_____Plastic dishes, cutlery unbroken
_____Clothes hooks above eye level

Music/Listening Center
_____Electric cords out of reach
_____Mercury battery equipment eliminated
_____Volume on headsets controlled

Water/Sand/Sensory Table
_____Water and sand at low levels
_____Spills cleaned up promptly
_____Broken, rusty or glass implements removed
_____Safety goggles used with sand

(Permission is granted by publisher to reproduce this page for evaluation and record keeping.)

General Room Conditions

Are you allowing concern for children's safety to overwhelm you? You shouldn't. Safety in your program should come naturally, almost intuitively, once you have started down the path of positive perspectives. Children's smiling faces, their endless enthusiasm and boundless energy—these should be the principal focus of your considerations. Keeping children safe should come as a subtle merging of safety with your thoughts and plans and actions on behalf of the youngsters. How is the classroom as you have set it up helping the children use it eagerly and safely? How can you make it better for them?

Walk into the classroom and take a look. Check the heating system first of all. Are there any exposed pipes along the walls? They should not be allowed unless they are thoroughly protected with non-asbestos insulation. What about radiators and space heaters? They should be sectioned off to prevent children's direct contact. All heating and ventilating equipment needs to be inspected before the cooling and heating seasons begin by a licensed contractor. As a teacher you may not be responsible for having this done, but you should contact whoever is responsible to make sure all is in order, including no harmful emissions from heating equipment. Portable electric or kerosene heaters are generally prohibited by fire codes or insurance regulations. Fans can be used only if they are inaccessible to children. (American Academy of Pediatrics, 2002, p. 199)

Next check the walls, cupboards, and furniture for peeling paint. Children often pick off pieces and put them in their mouths. Be sure all such surfaces are sanded and refinished with lead-free paint. Remove and repair any broken furniture. Check room dividers for splintery surfaces and have them refinished. Do not wait until someone's hand is pinched or receives a splinter. Put yourself in the place of an active child. Would you get hurt if you stumbled against the sharp corner of a room divider? You may need to tape padding onto all sharp corners.

Look down at your feet. Torn or uneven rugs and carpeting cause tripping. Adults may notice such wrinkles in rugs and step over them, but children often move too quickly to be aware of such hazards. Area rugs should have nonskid backing. Loop pile carpeting is especially good because it retains its appearance and is easily accessible for wheelchairs. In eating and art areas where spills are likely, washable floor coverings are more practical. (Fye and Mumpower, 2001, p. 18) A simple checklist such as Figure 2.3 can remind you to check on these elements of safety from time to time, and make necessary corrections.

FIGURE 2.3

Room Conditions Safety Checklist

_____Exposed pipes covered with non-asbestos insulation
_____Radiators and space heaters sectioned off from children
_____Portable electric and kerosene heaters removed
_____Peeling paint sanded down and refinished
_____Broken furniture removed and repaired
_____Splintery surfaces on wood sanded down
_____Sharp corners of room dividers padded
_____Torn or wrinkled carpeting removed or repaired

How Can You Make Learning Centers Accessible?

Young children need easy access to all of the learning centers in order to use them safely and independently. First of all they need to recognize what is available by the way you have the centers arranged. Are they pulled out from against the walls and sectioned off from one another? Open undivided learning centers against walls encourage children's chaotic running in the wide open middle space. On the other hand, rooms crowded with too many centers and no open aisles encourage pushing, shoving, and exclamations of "I was here first!" Room dividers need to be low enough for teachers to monitor the entire room, but high enough for children to experience privacy in each center. As Fye and Mumpower (2001) note: "When children move from center to center, they experience separate spaces, while the teacher views the area as one room divided into sections." (p. 22) Move through the room as a child in a wheelchair or on crutches might, and see if the aisles are spacious enough, the entrances to learning centers wide enough, and the centers themselves roomy enough to allow access but prevent crowding.

How Can You Encourage Children's Safe Use of Learning Centers?

Children learn best through on-the-spot experiences. In other words, giving admonishments ahead of time about what not to do in a learning center may be lost on youngsters who have not yet figured out how to use the materials in the first place. For example, children in the beginning stages of unit block building will be constructing flat walls and roads, not tall towers. Rules against building too high will be lost on them at first. Instead, you can unobtrusively observe what children are doing with materials and equipment in all of the centers. If materials are being misused, find a positive way to redirect children's use of them. Some teachers read appropriate children's picture books to individuals or small groups when things get out of hand to help them see things from a more acceptable point of view. Then have children develop simple rules.

41

Children in one science center often let the pet guinea pig Whiskers out of his cage to run around the classroom freely. Then they chased after him, running into other centers, bumping into other children's toys, and sometimes even knocking a child down. The teacher decided to call these particular children together to listen to a story about two pet guinea pigs who got loose in a house.

Books with Learning Center Themes

John Willy and Freddy McGee (Meade, 1998)

John Willy and Freddy McGee are two little guinea pigs who escape from their cage because the door is open and they are bored. They scurry, scoot, and scamper through the home where they live, knocking over toys and marble games and finally climbing up onto a pool table. Here they have the time of their lives ducking into the pockets and scurrying through the tunnels inside the pool table, until a cat climbs up on the table and smacks the balls into the pockets and down into the tunnels where the guinea pigs are scampering. They manage to escape being bonked by the rolling balls, and finally scurry back to their cage—but the door is still open.

The children in the listening group can discuss what is good and what is not so good about this adventure for the guinea pigs, for the cat, and for the people who live in the house. Then they will be ready to discuss their own situation: to decide what is good and not so good about their own guinea pig and the children in the other centers. Can they help to formulate rules or a method for playing with their guinea pig yet keeping him out of the other centers?

Click, Clack, Moo Cows That Type (Cronin, 2000)

Here is the right book to read to children who are fighting over use of the typewriter in the writing center. Farmer Brown's cows have found an old typewriter in the barn and type him a note telling him they want electric blankets because the barn is so cold at night. After an exchange of angry notes he finally gives in, but now the ducks have the typewriter and they want a diving board in the pond! Can your listeners find a way to use their typewriter without squabbling?

Henry Builds a Cabin (Johnson, 2002)

As birds build nests in the woods Henry builds a cabin from scratch, but his friends who come to watch him think it is too small to eat in, too dark to read in, and too small to dance in. Have children from the woodworking center sit close as you read this story to see how Henry is using his tools: an ax, a drill, a saw, and a hammer. Does he use them safely? Does his house turn out to be too small? How do they plan to use their own tools?

Lizzy's Do's and Don'ts (Harper, 2002)

The theme of this clever story is Lizzy's complaint that all her mother ever says is DON'T. Many of the don'ts are concerned with safety in the home and yard such as don't climb in trees containing bees, and don't try to reach what's out of reach. Lizzy turns the tables by using don't on her mother such as: don't act too tough, don't huff and puff. But they both realize there must be a better word to use, and they find finally it: DO!

Can the children help you rephrase the safety rules for each of your learning centers in a positive "DO-like" manner? The Learning Center Safety Checklist (see Figure 2.2) may help you. For instance, instead of telling Brandon: "Don't build that tower so high!" You might say: "Build your tower only as high as the top of your head." Instead of telling Kayla: "Don't take that sharp pencil out of the writing center!" You could say: "Please keep your pencil in the writing center, Kayla." Rather than telling Jesse: "Don't take that riding truck into the block center!" You might say: "You can ride your truck over in the aisle between the centers, Jesse." Or instead of saying: "Stop splashing water out of the water table, Tyrell!" You could say: "Let's drain some of the water out of the water table, so it doesn't splash out so easily, Tyrell."

No, David! (Shannon, 1998)

Here is another simple story, humorously illustrated, with a mother constantly telling her child "no,"—this one with a boy as its victim. (No wonder young children learn the word "no" so early and use it so often!) Finally, in the end the mother calls David into her arms and says: "Yes, Davey, I love you!" Challenge the children to listen for use of the word "no" in their classroom. Can they then think of saying the same thing in a positive way?

BATHROOM SAFETY

Slippery floors are one of the most common causes of bathroom injuries because of falls. You should check the bathroom floors from time to time during the day. Clean them promptly when there are spills. Sinks and toilets need to be cleaned and disinfected daily, and bathroom floors mopped. You may not be responsible for the initial cleaning, but you need to check to make sure it has been done. Bathroom cleaning supplies and disinfectants should be kept in a locked cabinet away from children.

The bathroom itself should be entered from the classroom with a door children can open easily from both sides. A minimum of one sink and one flush toilet is required for every 10 preschool children, but a minimum of two toilets per group is preferable when the group size approaches 10. Doors should be removed from stalls. Toilets and sinks should be child-sized. If the sinks are too tall, a stable step platform for children to stand on can be used with slip-proof steps and platform surface. If the bathroom is located outside the classroom, a staff member should accompany a child who needs to use it. Water temperatures should be at least 60 and no hotter than 120 degrees F. You can control the hot water temperature by turning down the water heater. Mark the faucets with hot and cold symbols in red and blue. (American Academy of Pediatrics, 2002, pp. 238–240).

Safety in the bathroom is sometimes influenced by children's personal bathroom habits. If children are new to the program they may not know what is expected of them initially. Although they learn quickly from their peers, young children also need to know what you expect. Find out if the children are used to being in a bathroom with other children. If they are not, you may need to accede to their feelings at first until they are used to the program and the other children. Talk to newcomers about what they can do. Can they handle their clothing, clean themselves, and wash their hands by themselves? You may need to go into the bathroom with them at first to get them started. Other children may need to be reminded about what the bathroom is for, and why playing with water in the bathroom is not acceptable. Use the Bathroom Safety Checklist in Figure 2.4 to appraise the safety of your own bathroom.

FIGURE 2.4

Bathroom Safety Checklist

_____Sinks clean, toilets flushed
_____Floors clean; mopped daily
_____Stands, stools sturdy, slip-proof
_____Cleaning and disinfecting materials locked up
_____Faucets labeled hot and cold
_____Water temperature under 120 degrees
_____Liquid soap, paper towels accessible

Book with a Bathroom Theme

Toilet Tales (Von Konigslow, 1985)

This comically illustrated story tells why big boys and girls can use the toilet and why animals like elephants, lions, snakes, and beavers cannot. A humorous story like this can help to relieve most of the tension some children may have about using the toilet. (Beaty, 2002, p. 111)

If you are unable to obtain any of the books listed in this chapter, try making up your own stories about puppets using the bathroom or learning centers correctly or incorrectly. Storytelling is simple if you do it with a puppet or stuffed animal, and you will soon have the children's undivided attention. Then they can tell their own stories about what the puppet or animal should have done.

ENTRANCES AND EXITS

Among the safest places in the program should be the steps, entrance door, and hall leading to the classroom. Often this is not the case. Check the entrance to your building from the point of view of a child entering or exiting. If there are stairs, are they covered with a nonskid material having no tears or wrinkles? Are the steps sturdy and unbroken? Because of their constant use, and because the entrance may be exposed to outside elements such as rain, sleet or snow, stairs and stair coverings often deteriorate over time. They need to be repaired as soon as this condition is evident. Do not wait for someone to trip and fall.

What about stair railings? Can children ages three, four, and five reach and hold onto the railings easily. If railings are at adult height, a second lower railing should be installed for the children's use. Facilities that include children with physical disabilities must have ramps as well as steps. The corridors, passageways, and aisles leading to each exit need to be kept free of materials and furniture that would prevent clear access. Cutout footprints mounted on the floor as a trail can guide children to exits. The standard for exits in child care facilities is as follows:

> Each building or structure, new or old, shall be provided with a minimum of two exits, at different sides of the building or home, leading to an open space at ground level. If the basement in a small family child care home is being used, one exit must lead directly to the outside. Exits shall be unobstructed, allowing occupants to escape to an outside door or stair enclosure in case of fire or other emergency. (American Academy of Pediatrics, 2002, p. 194)

Arrival and Departure

No matter how physically safe you have made your entrances and exits, there is always another safety element to consider. As soon as you put people in the picture, things change. The daily arrival and departure of children and their parents is often a confused occurrence with the possibility for unexpected things to happen. When children arrive by school bus, they may want to hurry into the building in an excited crowd, stumbling up steps or pushing the children in front of them. It is necessary for bus drivers to help such youngsters calm down, slow down, and climb down the bus steps carefully. They can then proceed single-file into the building where an adult staff member awaits them at the door or head of the steps.

When parents or family members drop off their children it is necessary for the parent to enter the classroom with the child and to make contact with the teacher. When this meeting and greeting takes place outside the building, extra precaution needs to be focused on the safety of the children. As Taylor (2002) notes: "Young children have been known to wander, try unexpected things, or even steer younger siblings into dangerous situations because parents and teachers are momentarily distracted." (p. 328)

Departures at the end of the day may be accompanied by the same kind of confusion among teachers, children, families, and bus drivers if safety concerns have not been anticipated and accommodated. For example, who is legally designated to pick up the child? A list of authorized individuals must be at the check-out area daily. As Taylor notes: "It is the teacher's responsibility—not the child's—to release the child to an authorized person." (p. 328) Children may recognize and want to go with the person who appears, but because of custody problems, this person may not be an authorized one.

Teachers can help the situation by following a regular departure routine with the children that addresses their emotional, physical, and personal safety needs. A daily "dismissal circle" gives children the opportunity to express these concerns. One teacher found that at the beginning of the year children who rode the bus were worried about the driver's ability to get them home. The teacher was able to arrange for a bus to come early to the school and for the children to explore it, sitting in seats, trying on seat belts, and putting the windows up and down. The driver explained how she was able to get each child home. (Fox, 1999, pp. 12–14)

Children also expressed the need to use the restroom before they got home, so time was arranged during the dismissal circle for them to use it. Children who waited for parents to pick them up were also worried at first that their parents would forget them. Teachers tried to alleviate this problem by reading stories about parents picking up their children.

Books with a Departure Theme

Will You Come Back for Me? (Tompert, 1988)

When Suki first goes to a child care program she is worried that her mother won't come back for her. They talk about this ahead of time, and her mother cuts out a big red paper heart with her name in the middle, then tears it in two. The mother shows how she will leave half of her heart at the child care center. But not for long. She puts the heart back together to show how it will be when she comes to get Suki. Suki understands and calms down. Talk to small groups of children concerning how they feel about staying in the class, leaving at the end of the day, and getting back with their parents.

My Somebody Special (Weeks, 2002)

In this brightly illustrated book all of the children and adults in the preschool are animals who play and talk as humans. Double page illustrations with four brief lines of rhyming text tell how "Our busy day/ is almost through./ Somebody special/ is coming for you." As the children continue their activities of painting, playing with riding toys, listening to stories, eating snacks, dressing up, and building with blocks, their parents come one by one to pick them up. Finally, only one little animal-child is left—very worried and forlorn. But then the door opens and his mother appears. Have the children look carefully at the pictures as you reread this story and choose which animal-child they would like to be. Can they tell you why?

THIS CHAPTER'S ROLE

Teachers can promote safety within the classroom by setting up the learning centers with safety in mind. A Learning Center Safety Checklist helps to alert teachers to the elements of safety they need to be concerned with in each center. The size, physical arrangement, materials in use, and whether water or electricity are needed in the centers are considered. Children's actual use of each center is just as important as teachers observe children in action and make necessary adjustments. General room conditions such as heating, carpeting, walls, and corners can be checked and made safe. Spacing the learning centers to make them accessible for everyone including physically challenged children is addressed. Encouraging children's safe use of centers through stories and follow-up activities are positive methods for ensuring safety. Bathroom safety is principally concerned with injuries because of falls on slippery floors or from sink platforms. Arrival and departure of children through safe entrances and exits concludes the chapter discussing not only physical issues, but also the emotional and personal safety needs of the children.

WHAT HAVE YOU LEARNED FROM THIS CHAPTER?

1. How does setting up the learning centers relate to safety? Be specific.

2. What safety problems might occur in a book center?

3. How should you set up a computer so it is safe for young children's use?

4. Why should you not use small beads and counters in a manipulative/math center?

5. What kind of scissors should you have in the art center? How should they be used?

6. What should you do if children climb up on chairs to build really high block towers?

7. What safety features should you look for in large motor equipment for indoor use?

8. Would you include a woodworking center in your classroom? Why or why not?

9. How can you encourage safe use of all the learning centers?

10. What two books would you use to help children feel safe in the classroom?

11. How would you use them?

HOW CAN YOU APPLY WHAT YOU HAVE LEARNED?

1. Use the Learning Center Safety Checklist to check on safety features in your classroom. What changes do you need to make?

2. Set up a science/discovery center in your classroom with safety as well as your curriculum in mind. How do you your children use it?

3. Use the Bathroom Safety Checklist for a week especially when children are using the bathroom. What changes might you need to make?

4. Set up a new child's private area in your classroom. How do you do this and how to the children use it?

5. Use the Room Conditions Safety Checklist. Do you find anything that needs changing? How will you take care of this?

6. Describe your building and classroom entrance. What can you do to make entering the building and classroom easier and safer for the children?

7. Describe the arrival of the children on a typical morning. What safety factors in and outside the classroom need to be addressed? How can you respond to these?

8. Describe the departure of the children on a typical day. What physical, personal, and emotional factors affect the children? How would you handle these?

9. Read a book with a learning center theme and follow up with an activity that helps children make one of their learning centers safer. Describe what happens.

10. If you could purchase one piece of equipment to help the classroom become a safer place for the children, what would it be? How would you or they use it?

REFERENCES

American Academy of Pediatrics. (2002). *Caring for our children.* Elk Grove Village, IL: Author.

Beaty, J. J. (2002). *Observing development of the young child.* Upper Saddle River, NJ: Merrill/Prentice Hall.

Bunnett, R., & Davis, N. L. (1997). Getting to the heart of the matter. *Child Care Information Exchange, 114,* 42–44.

Fox, J. E. (1999). "It's time to go home!" Reframing dismissal routines. *Dimensions of Early Childhood, 27*(3), 11–15.

Fye, M.A.S., & Mumpower, J. P. (2001). Lost in space? Design learning areas for today. *Dimensions of Early Childhood, 29*(2), 16–22.

Isbell, R. (1995). *The complete learning center book.* Beltsville, MD: Gryphon House.

Lay-Dopyera, M., & Dopyera, J. (1990). *Becoming a teacher of young children.* New York: McGraw-Hill.

Stoll, B. H. (2000). *A to Z health and safety in the child care setting.* St. Paul, MN: Redleaf Press.

Taylor, B. J. (2002). *Early childhood program management: People and procedures.* Upper Saddler River, NJ: Merrill/Prentice Hall.

SUGGESTED READINGS

Hearron, P. F., & Hildebrand, V. (2003). *Management of child development centers* (5th ed.). Upper Saddle River, NJ: Merrill/Prentice Hall.

Hendrick, J. (2003). *Total learning: Developmental curriculum for the young child* (6th ed.). Upper Saddle River, NJ: Merrill/Prentice Hall.

McLean, D. (2002). Helping Aaron navigate: Including children with physical disabilities. *Dimensions of Early Childhood, 30*(1), 9–16.

Sloane, M. W. (2000). Make the most of learning centers. *Dimensions of Early Childhood, 28*(1), 16–20.

CHILDREN'S BOOKS

Cronin, D. (2000). *Click, clack, moo cows that type.* New York: Simon & Schuster.

Harper, J. (2001). *Lizzy's do's and don'ts.* New York: HarperCollins.

Johnson, D. B. (2002). *Henry builds a cabin.* Boston: Houghton Mifflin.

Meade, H. (1998). *John Willy and Freddy McGee.* New York: Marshall Cavendish.

Shannon, D. (1998). *No, David!* New York: Blue Sky Press.

Tompert, A. (1988). *Will you come back for me?* Morton Grove, IL: Albert Whitman.

Von Konigslow, A.W. (1985). *Toilet tales.* Toronto: Annick.

Weeks, S. (2002). *My somebody special.* San Diego, CA: Harcourt, Inc.

Chapter 3

SAFETY: THE OUTDOOR CURRICULUM

PLAYGROUND SAFETY
STREET SAFETY
TRANSPORATION SAFETY
FIELD TRIPS

PLAYGROUND SAFETY

Children's playgrounds can be one of the most exciting learning areas of your program if they have been set up with safety in mind. Most of the safety hazards described in this chapter will not affect children if the playgrounds have been set up initially to address these problems, and maintained on a regular basis. The keys, then, to playground safety include:

- Safe environment
- Education of children
- Playground supervision
- Rules enforced consistently

Safe Environment

The environment includes the location of the playground, sectioned off by sturdy fencing from parking areas, roads, driveways, vehicles, and other outside activities; the size and location of playground equipment; the materials used in manufacturing the equipment; the materials used in cushioning the ground under the equipment; the size of the fall space around the equipment; and the space between the various pieces of equipment. Safety hazards in the environment itself include natural hazards such as trees with branches low enough for children to climb; rock walls; open bodies of water; ditches; and tripping hazards from roots, rocks, and low barriers separating equipment. Safety hazards in playground equipment include: heights of equipment, protrusion and entanglement hazards, entrapment in openings, pinching and sharp edge hazards.

A number of agencies produce guidelines, handbooks, brochures, and checklists relating to playground safety including: United States Consumer Product Safety Commission (1-800-638-2772); National Recreation and Park Association (703-858-0784); National Program for Playground Safety (1-800-554-7529); and Health Consultants for Child Care (952-472-3915).

Slides

One of the first areas children head for as they stream out of the classroom and onto the playground is often the slide area. What a thrill to climb up the steps and skim down the sliding board with a swish and a jolt at the bottom. Slides come in a wide variety of types, sizes, and materials. Choose the right kind for your program according to the ages of the children, the size of the playground, and the number of children who will be using it. Free standing slides are not as popular nor as safe as multiple access slides with steps and ladders going up, one or more platforms or decks, and perhaps a fire pole, in addition to the slides, coming down—often more than one slide.

Because injuries due to falls are the most common slide hazard, sliding equipment needs to be placed in a play zone or fall zone covered under and around the equipment with loose fill material such as splinter-free shredded wood mulch or wood chips, sand or pea gravel, or rubbery mats and tiles to a depth of 12 inches, and with a retaining barrier to contain the material. The loose material should be free of standing water and raked daily so it won't become compacted at the ends of slides. Materials that are not safe under play equipment include carpeting, gym mats, blacktop, concrete, grass or dirt. If your program includes children ages three and under, pea gravel may be a choking hazard or they may put it in their noses or ears. (Stoll, 2000, p. 76)

Slides for preschool children should be four feet or less in height, the lower the height, the safer the slide. The fall zone needs to be six feet out from the edges of the equipment in all directions. The exit from the end of the slide should be not more than 11 inches off the ground. Be sure the ground surface is level at the end of the slide, and not hard and compacted or trampled into a hole that fills with water when it rains.

If slides are metal they need to be painted or galvanized. Metal slides pose the problem of hot surfaces that can burn in summer and cold surfaces that may stick to skin in winter. Plastic slides are more popular these days and need less maintenance.

Platforms at the tops of slides should be at least as wide as the slide and 15 inches in length for preschoolers. Open platforms need railings that are high enough to keep youngsters from climbing over them, with railings having vertical slats close enough together that heads cannot be entrapped. The bottom of the railing should also come close to the platform itself so that children cannot slide under it. As you know or will soon learn, young children try out everything in every way possible—especially in ways not designed for the equipment. Be sure to check to make sure there is no gap between the platform and sliding surface where clothing might catch or fingers might become pinched.

Swings

Swings are also a favorite piece of equipment for preschool children. Swings need a front and back fall zone which is equal to their height plus two times the height of the swing, as well as six feet to either side. There should be no more than two swings to a bay. The seats for preschoolers should be pliable rubber or plastic belts, or bucket seats for children younger than three. Cushioning material in the fall zone under and around the swings should be the same as that for slides. Because of the danger of moving swings hitting unaware children, they need to be placed away from high activity areas. Fall zones for equipment should not overlap. In fact, there needs to be a minimum of 12 feet between any large play structures such as swings, slides, and climbers. Swings should not be a part of other play equipment as is the case with many backyard sets. They should be separately anchored firmly in the ground with concrete footers buried at least 12 inches below the playing surface.

Climbing and Stationary Equipment

Large pieces of stationary equipment are particularly popular on today's playgrounds. Made of wood or plastic, children use them for climbing, crawling, sliding, swinging hand-over-hand across horizontal ladders, crossing swinging bridges, climbing up or down rope ladders or cargo nets, and sliding down fire poles. They may consist of shaded platforms at different levels, a plastic playhouse, steps or stairs going up and down, tube slides, wave slides, corkscrew climbers, and round openings leading to crawl tunnels. These linked activities provide exciting challenges for a number of children at a time. Those who may not participate in movement activities often carry out dramatic play scenarios in the under-deck play spaces. Other stand-alone climbing equipment for preschoolers includes small dome climbers, tent climbers, ring climbers, and the so-called "squirrel house" with its maze of colorful bars, holes for handholds, and a fire pole inside. Traditional metal monkey bar sets are seldom to be seen.

Once again such equipment should be cushioned underneath and around with at least 12 inches of loose fill material in the fall zone, which is projected out six feet all around. Handrails and climbing bars should be one to one and a quarter inches in diameter. Rungs of overhead horizontal ladders should be more than nine inches apart. Check for trapping hazards in railings, rope ladders, and cargo nets. Rope ladders and nets should have either very small openings that heads cannot go through, or very large openings that will not entrap heads. Check also for protruding bolt ends which should be covered, as well as sharp points and edges which should be filed down. Wooden equipment may also deteriorate with time, may become splintered, and will need to be sanded down. (United States Consumer Product Safety Commission, 1997). Why do children climb? Readdick and Park (1998) tell us:

> Climbing is a central motor achievement for the developing child.
> Children, in fact, learn to climb *before* they begin to walk and
> continue to climb throughout their early childhood years. Besides
> the fairly obvious fact that children can be badly injured doing it,
> most children climb with joy and skill, demonstrating an irresistible
> urge for independence, competence, and mastery. (p. 14)

Whatever the reason, we need to make sure that the climbing equipment we provide is not only developmentally appropriate for children ages three to five, but also safe. The exercise of children's arms, hands, shoulders, legs, and feet that climbing provides is well worth the time and energy we must expend in selecting the best equipment, installing it properly, inspecting it carefully, and keeping up with its maintenance.

Sandboxes and Water Tables

Sandboxes are even more popular outside than inside. They need to be constructed to permit drainage. They also need to be covered when not in use with covers that permit light and air to circulate to allow natural cleaning of the sand. (Stoll, 2000, p. 76) Sand and water toys can be kept outside in a storage box or shed or carried out from the classroom. Don't forget the safety goggles. The number of pairs you provide determines the number of children who can play in sand at once.

Teachers who provide sandboxes and water tables on their playgrounds always note that the children's play seems different outside. Stephenson (2002) suggests that "outdoor activities are more open-ended, allowing children to become more engrossed and less dependent on adults." (p. 12) It is as if children feel that the outdoors belongs to them. It is less structured and controlled than the indoors of the classroom, and they take grand advantage of this fact by running freely, shouting loudly, and joining exuberantly in whatever activity they feel like at the moment. Teachers need to provide goggles at the sand table and aprons at the water table, but other than this, they should keep hands off. Let the children be in control so long as they keep within safety bounds and social play constraints, i.e., where they don't hurt themselves, hurt others, or damage materials.

Wheeled Equipment

Another important part of the playground is the sidewalk, trike path, or blacktop area for use of wheeled vehicles. Children love to pedal, push, and pull tricycles, scooters, and wagons round and round the designated pathways. Be sure you have enough of several kinds vehicles for several children at once. Three-wheel scooters are safer than two-wheel scooters, but it is good to have both as a challenge for children at different skill levels. All of the wheeled toys should conform to American Society for Testing Materials (ASTM) standards and the U. S. Consumer Product Safety Commission (CPSC) guidelines. Be sure to check catalogs or stores for such conformation before purchasing these toys. Different sizes of trikes may be necessary for the different ages of children in your class. Also consider providing child-size safety helmets for the riders. Tandem or chariot trikes are other popular vehicles for turn-taking experiences and giving another child a ride. Keep an eye out for possible conflicts when passengers try to be the driver.

What about children with impaired physical abilities? Use your ingenuity to find ways to include all children in as many playground activities as possible. As Flynn and Kief (2002) point out:

> Teachers may think at first that a riding toy is not appropriate for a child who is blind or has low vision because of her inability to see where she is going. However, a beeper can be placed on the back of the tricycle of another child and the child who is blind plays "follow the leader" with the child whose tricycle has been adapted. (p. 21)

You will soon find that everyone wants to pretend to be blind so they too can "follow the leader!" Put a blindfold over their eyes if they want and let them try.

Inspection and Maintenance

Whenever the playground is to be used by the children, a staff member must spend time inspecting the grounds and equipment for possible safety problems. The Playground Safety Checklist (see Figure 3.1) can be used as a check off sheet to make sure everything is in order. In addition, an established schedule of inspection for preventative maintenance on equipment should be set up at the beginning of the year. Look for corrosion, weathering, or rot on equipment. Is equipment still securely anchored? Does it have any splinters or loose or protruding parts? Repairs should be made promptly after being reported. Broken equipment should be sectioned off and not used until it is fixed. Keep a list of inspections as well as any accident reports of children's injuries on equipment.

FIGURE 3.1

Playground Safety Checklist

_____Playground enclosed with fence
_____Debris, litter, broken glass, animal waste removed
_____Mushrooms, poisonous plants, berries, removed
_____Tripping hazards such as pot holes, roots, rocks corrected
_____Proper cushioning material under and around equipment
_____Loose cushioning material free of standing water
_____Fall zones adequate, equipment zones widely separated
_____Ropes on swings and rope climbers not frayed or broken
_____Slides and other metal equipment not rusted
_____Wooden equipment not splintery
_____Landing pits refilled, cushioning material raked
_____Loose nuts, bolts tightened, covered
_____Broken railings fixed; no spaces for body-part entrapment
_____Equipment anchored properly with buried footers
_____Sand in boxes clean, no foreign matter
_____Toys and equipment size-appropriate for preschoolers

Equipment Not Recommended

A great deal of playground equipment for sale or in use is not recommended for children ages three to five. For example, do not purchase or use heavy swing sets made of animal characters. Even with proper belt-type seats, swings are a dangerous piece of equipment for young children to maneuver around. Many pay little attention to the backward motion of swings and may be hit by them. Such heavy animal swings can do real damage. Other swinging devices that are unacceptable for this age group include swings with board seats, multiple occupancy to-and-fro swings, rope swings, and swinging exercise rings.

Other equipment not recommended for preschool outdoor use includes trampolines, trapeze bars, merry-go-rounds, see-saws, and full arch climbers. Much of the climbing equipment, swings, and slides on public playgrounds is too large and unsafe for preschool children. Stationary plastic animals on springs are not recommended because of falling and pinching potential. Of course, such young children will want to investigate the spring underneath and may get pinched.

Merry-go-rounds are too difficult for most preschool children to use safely. Getting on and off when merry-go-rounds are moving can throw children to the ground. Trying to stay on when they are spinning fast is beyond the capabilities of most preschoolers. The see-saw or teeter-totter is another dangerous piece of equipment for children this young. A young child can be thrown off even a small see-saw when the child at the lower end jumps off. The safe use of a see-saw is still too complex for most three- and four-year-olds to learn.

Create-a-Playground

For programs with no playground equipment at all, except for the public playground nearby, please consider not using the public playground if it contains equipment too large or too dangerous for your children. Instead, you can create your own playground by substituting appropriate materials to promote large motor exercise somewhere on your own grounds. Use balls, jump ropes, hula hoops, cloth play tunnels, tin can stilts, and sidewalk chalk games. Throw balls into holes cut out of appliance boxes. Bring out mats and a balance beam from indoors. Set up a temporary obstacle course using tires, milk crates, large plastic snap cubes, small cable spools, card tables, carpet remnants, appliance boxes, trash can covers, and plastic trash cans themselves with the bottoms cut out. (Griffin and Rinn, 1998, pp. 19–23). Have a temporary wading pool in warm weather. Use yours and your children's ingenuity. They may like it even better than a commercial playground.

Education of Children

How do you get young children to act safely on the playground without strong admonitions and threats? Without long lists of do's and don'ts? We want children to feel free out-of-doors—to be able to run and shout and jump for joy. Too many rules spoil their fun, and may not in the long run keep them any safer.

The trick is to get the children to consider themselves a part of the rule-making, behavior-managing process. Keep the terms understandable and interesting to them, and they may buy into them. For instance, instead of telling children what not to do, ask them to help you develop some "playground manners" that all of you will follow—you included. "Manners" means treating others with consideration, that is, not shoving or pushing on the slide set, or trying to cut ahead of someone in line. It means taking turns and waiting your turn without squabbling; not throwing sand or splashing water on others; not running in back of swings; looking before you leap; and others.

At the beginning of the year when children are still new to the program take a small group at a time out on the playground and ask them to walk around with you to each piece of equipment. Ask them to think of what playground manners they should practice when they use the slide, the swings, the climbing equipment, the sandbox, the water table, and the trikes, so they won't hurt themselves or someone else. Then have them try each piece of equipment and see if the playground manners they mentioned really work. Young children are very perceptive. They may notice something you never thought of. For instance, Melissa pointed out to her teacher: "Kyle is going to get his jacket drawstring caught on the top of that slide, if he slides down flat like that. Maybe it will choke him." Yes, good point. It would then be imperative for you to ask all parents to remove drawstrings on clothing.

Kim commented: "If we climb up the slide from the bottom like Jake is doing, maybe somebody sliding down from the top will crash into him." Yes, again. "How should we handle that?" you can ask your group. They may decide it is okay to climb up from the bottom if the child on top waits until the bottom child leaves the slide. But he should ask first. Rules are best when made on the spot by the children themselves.

Once back in the classroom you can read a book about playground activities to your small group while another staff member introduces another small group to the playground equipment just as you have done.

Books with Playground Themes

Chicken Chickens (Gorbachev, 2001)

Here is just the book for introducing preschool children to the playground. Have the children sit close to see the pictures while you read. Mother Hen takes her two little chickens to the playground for the very first time. The little chickens are scared to see so many animals playing on so much equipment: dogs on teeter totters, pigs on the merry-go-round, a rabbit riding a trike, turtles in the sandbox, and cats on the swings. The dogs invite the two chickens on the teeter totter, but they say they're too little. The pigs invite the chicken children to ride on the merry-go-round, but they say they might get dizzy. The cats invite the chickens to swing, but they say they might fall off. When the mice who are littler than the chickens urge them to slide, they finally give in and climb up the ladder. But at the top they are still too scared to slide down until a beaver lets them ride on his tail. Next time up they feel they can slide down by themselves, and they do. Can your listeners relate to this book? Ask them what they would do in each case. Ask them how the animals were practicing playground manners on each piece of equipment. Does anyone note there is no railing around the slide platform?

It is important for you to obtain well written, handsomely illustrated, but also useful books like this for your classroom. If the children like it they will ask you to read it over and over. Afterwards they will spend a great deal of time looking at and commenting on the pictures. If you have no budget for books, borrow this one from your public library. They will be able to obtain it for you, even if it is not on their own shelves.

Duck on a Bike (Shannon, 2002)

Your children will be riding trikes, not bikes like the talking animals in this book. But no matter. When Duck first takes a ride on the farm boy's bike he rides proudly past each of the animals in the barnyard, and they think to themselves something about a duck on a bike just as the sheep does: "He's going to hurt himself if he's not careful." But later when a whole bunch of kids ride out to visit the boy and park their bikes outside, all the animals in the barnyard decide to copy Duck and take a ride. Outstanding close-up illustrations make this book a favorite of all who see it. What do your listeners think about animals riding bikes? Can they pretend to be animals when they ride their own trikes? What playground manners should they follow?

Down By the Cool of the Pool (Mitton, 2001)

If you have a wading pool, you might want to read this cumulative tale in which frog invites each animal to dance like he does. But duck flaps, pig wiggles, sheep stamps, dog frisks, goat butts, pony prances, donkey drums, and cow capers. When they all do their dance together they slip into the pool with a splash. Large enticing illustrations will attract your listeners, but is this a book that promotes playground manners? Ask the children how they should behave in their wading pool. Have each one choose one of the animal's motions outside the pool and then step carefully into the pool.

Playground Supervision

At least two members of the teaching staff should accompany the children out on the playground. If more than one class wants to use the playground at the same time, you must work out a schedule so that classes can alternate. Too many children at once makes it difficult to supervise, causes congestion on the equipment, and creates situations that can cause injury to children.

In hot sunny weather, the supervisors must make sure metal equipment such as slides are not too hot for children's use. When the temperature is above 75 degrees supervisors should have the children slow down, take 15 minute breaks, and drink plenty of water to avoid dehydration. Loose clothing, hats, and sunscreen should be used by everyone. Are there shaded areas where children and adults can get out of the sun for awhile? If not, bring out beach umbrellas. When temperatures rise above 84 degrees, take the children inside.

As a playground supervisor you should also cut short play and bring the children inside when air pollution becomes high, during dust storms and electrical storms, as well as during extremes of high temperature and humidity. During cold weather children can play outside for brief periods if they are completely covered with warm clothing, mittens, hats, and boots. In this case it is metal surfaces that may need to be avoided so skin will not stick to them.

Before children go outside one of the supervisors needs to make an overall check of the playground using the Playground Safety Checklist (Figure 3.1), to make sure everything is cleaned up and in safe condition. The two supervisors should spread out across the area where children are playing to keep in view the most children at a time and be able to communicate with them. Make sure that all of the children are visible to at least one of the supervisors at all times.

Playground supervisors should be aware of the fact that this is not a recreation period for them. They need to be active supervisors. If they interact with a few children, they need to make it brief so they can return to their principal function of overseeing all of the children. Children's accidents and injuries tend to happen when no one is looking or paying attention to situations such as too many children on top of a slide, or a child running behind a moving swing, or children throwing sand at one another. Playground duty is not a time to socialize with another adult or child.

Carry a cell phone with you to phone in emergency situations. If a dangerous animal or person should appear, signal the children to assemble quickly around you and take them inside. You may want to carry a whistle as a signal. If a child needs to be taken inside by one of the two supervisors, signal the other children to come closer to you by starting a game with them such as follow-the-leader, or have them sit down and listen to a story, sing a song, or do a finger play until the other adult returns. Teach the children ahead of time what your signals mean. If classroom volunteers and student teachers are used as playground supervisors, they need to be advised of their role before they go outside.

Rules Enforced Consistently

How can you make sure all of the children follow safety rules without your being severe and harsh? Think about the rules you require the children to follow within the classroom. You remember they are more concerned with "do's" than "don'ts" as discussed in Chapter 2. The same kinds of rules need to be formed by the teachers and children and enforced on the playground. They should be simple and few in number. You will be talking in terms of "playground manners" as previously described. You may need to jot down the most important of these manners ahead of time, to remind you of what has been discussed and agreed upon by you and the children. Then all the adults who supervise the playground should agree on how they will enforce these rules.

Some playground manners that one teacher and her children devised always state something positive first:

- Running is good, but pushing is not.
- Running on the ground is good, but running up the slide is not.
- Taking turns is good, but cutting in is not.
- Throwing balls is good, but throwing sand is not.
- Look where you're going is the best.

The teacher and the staff repeated these rules so many times on the playground that everyone knew them by heart. Soon the children themselves were using the rules to remind their buddies how to act—or how not to act. They even taught these rules to new student teachers whenever they appeared on the outdoor scene

Another teacher kept track of the following simple rules she and the children had agreed on:

- <u>Ask before you take.</u> (They had problems of children grabbing other children's sand toys, trucks, and trikes.)
- <u>One child at a time</u>. (There were problems of too many children using the swinging bridge and horizontal ladder at the same time.)
- <u>Help your buddy</u>. (This rule seemed to stop conflicts between two children and get them to help one another instead of fighting.)

What if children continue abusing the rules anyway? How can you enforce them consistently? Once again, you and the children can agree on a consequence at the time you agree on the particular playground rule. Every group of children is different but most will accept the solution of giving a rule-breaker a second chance. Then if he or she continues ignoring the rule, you need to have the child come and sit by you for a moment while you talk about reason for having the "playground manner," and whether the child will agree to abide by it. Having the child go and sit somewhere far away is too much like using a "time out" chair outside. Time out by oneself is more like a punishment that makes the child angry and want to strike back, rather than a learning situation in which he understands why the rule was established.

When children have a part in devising their own playground manners and consequences they are more likely to follow them. Rules devised and enforced by teachers alone seem more like a calculated method of control over the children, rather than a concern for the children's safety. Yet behind all the playground manners and rules lies the common classroom limit of not letting children hurt themselves, hurt one another, or damage materials.

STREET SAFETY

Pedestrian Safety

Outdoor safety for preschool programs extends out much farther than the playground. Street safety is just as important for teachers to consider when children walk to and from school with parents or walk on field trips with teachers. Because young children are often impulsive and drivers are sometimes inattentive, it is essential that enough classroom time as necessary be spent on alerting children to traffic dangers and safe pedestrian behavior at the beginning of the year. As noted by Owens and Patterson (2001):

> Children's safety is a significant aspect of early childhood education. Many practitioners are conscious of the dangers for young children in the traffic environment and are likely to see road safety education as an important area of responsibility. While parents are highly skilled in making traffic-related decisions themselves, they may not be effective in teaching children these skills without additional support.

If parents teach their children street safety from a negative perspective with "no's" and "don'ts," it is imperative for the preschool teaching staff to help children learn the positive aspects of actions that can and should be taken. For example, pedestrian safety for preschool children can include the following elements:

- Holding hands while walking
- Waiting to cross the street or road
- Using the pedestrian crossing
- Using traffic lights correctly
- Crossing the street or road with an adult

In a city environment children will need to learn about stopping at a curb, listening for oncoming traffic, looking both ways, pressing the "walk" button if there is one, and waiting for the walk sign to appear, or waiting for the stoplight to turn green, but making sure the cars have stopped before beginning to cross while holding hands with an adult. In a rural environment, children, with the help of an adult, will need to choose a safe place to cross, stop at the edge of the road, listen for on-coming traffic, look both ways, and cross cautiously holding hands with an adult.

Children should not cross the street alone until they are at least 10 years old. Their depth of perception is not as developed as an adult's so they have difficulty judging the speed and distance of on-coming cars. They also have limited peripheral vision, making it hard to notice cars turning from the side. In addition, their sense of hearing is not as well developed as an adults. Thus they may not be able to isolate the direction of a honking horn. (Settle & Price, 2000, p. 134)

Another problem with young children is their shortness. They assume that if they can see the car, truck, or SUV, then it can see them. But trucks and SUVs have trouble seeing young children, especially when they are backing up. Children need to be alerted to the danger of walking behind any vehicle. (Settle & Price, p. 134)

Children can learn these safety rules on-the-spot by practicing them in small groups outside with one of the classroom staff. They can learn to play on the playground or with supervision on the sidewalk near the building, if this is permitted, but not in the street or a driveway. Walk each child by the hand over to the crosswalk and make a big show of stopping and looking right and left before stepping off the curb. Show them how some cars turn right on red, so they must always check for cars coming around the corner before they try to cross. Talk to them about always walking across the street and not running; about always crossing the street at the corner and not jaywalking. Another day have each child lead you over to the crosswalk and tell you what to do—a good way to discover what the child has learned.

63

Driveways, garages, and parking lots can be especially dangerous places for young children who are hard for drivers to see because of their size. Ask parents to dress their children in bright outside clothing if they can. Have children walk from their car to the school building holding a parent's hand. If vehicles are backing up children must wait and not try to run behind them. Nor should they try to cross a street from between parked cars. When they are in parking lots children need to hold the hand of an adult, or if the adult's hands are full, then hold onto her clothing. You have probably noted that some children are more impulsive than others. Spend more time practicing street safety with them. When you are walking with children be sure to point out drivers who don't yield to pedestrians, making it imperative for them to wait and look before crossing a street.

Teachers also need to follow-up with classroom activities such as reading books about walking on the street and setting up the block center or sand table with little cars, trucks, people figures, and traffic signs for children to act out their own safety rules. In addition, community helpers such as police officers and school crossing guards can visit the classroom and demonstrate safety to the children.

Children take home what they learn in preschool. If the rules are simple and easy to remember, they will be repeating them to their parents when they are out on the street. In addition, be sure to include information on how you teach children about street safety in one of the parent meetings held early in the year, as well as in a parents' newsletter. Some pedestrian safety rules are listed in Figure 3.2.

FIGURE 3.2

Pedestrian Safety Rules

- Cross streets only at corner or crosswalk.
- Hold adult's hand when crossing street.
- Look both ways before crossing street.
- Wait for green light or walk sign.
- Walk only in front of vehicles.
- Hold adult's hand or clothing in parking lots.

Books with a Pedestrian Theme

Red Light, Green Light, Mama and Me (Best, 1995)

Lizzie walks to work with her mother through the city with its tall buildings and heavy traffic, down the steps to the subway, and up again walking tall and proud up the steps of the Downtown Public Library where her mother works. In this first person story Lizzie tells how she helps her mother during storytelling, how she eats a city picnic on the steps outside the library, makes bookmarks for everyone, and finally walks home again. Have your listeners pretend to be Lizzie as they go along the city sidewalks. Can they follow any of the safety rules they have learned?

Rap a Tap Tap: Here's Bojangles—Think of That! (Dillon & Dillon, 2002)

This exuberantly illustrated book celebrates the legendary Bill Robinson as he tap dances his way down city streets, bringing pleasure and joy to the people he'd meet. "Rap a tap tap—think of that!" He dances past bus stops, fruit stands, fancy hotels, street musicians, crowds of laughing kids, fish markets, a bus with the sign "Listen Look" on its side, policemen, and street cleaners. Double page illustrations with a simple rhyming line at the bottom follow his gyrations. Have your children play follow-the-leader with stops and starts in the classroom as you read the book, and afterwards talk about any street safety elements they note in the pictures or in your game.

Somewhere in Africa (Mennen & Daly, 1990)

Ashraf lives in Africa, but not the Africa of lions in golden grass or crocodiles in muddy rivers. He lives in a city at the tip of the great African continent, and this is the story of his walk through the city streets with blinking traffic lights and noisy cars, past the singing fruit seller and smiling flower sellers and street musicians, to the library where he renews his favorite book, and back home again. Have children sit close to see if they can find and follow Ashraf in the pictures. How would they maneuver safely through the streets if they were Ashraf? Do they see any dangers?

TRANSPORTATION SAFETY

Many children come to school in cars driven by parents or neighbors. Others may ride the school bus. Everyone will have a chance to ride a school bus on a field trip. Because all of the children will be riding in a vehicle at one time or another your safety program should include facts about safe operation of transportation vehicles, and children's behavior in the vehicles.

In cars, children under 80 pounds and four feet, nine inches tall need to ride in child restraint systems—safety seats and seat belts—secured in back seats only. A booster safety seat needs to be used when the child has outgrown the convertible seat used for toddlers but is too small to fit properly in a vehicle safety belt. (American Academy of Pediatrics, 2002, pp. 274–275) Because head-on collisions cause the greatest number of serious injuries, children sitting in the back seat of the vehicle are farthest away from the impact and less likely to be injured. Encourage drivers to carry cell phones to be used in case of an emergency. Cars that transport children also need to be air conditioned in hot weather and heated in cold. Since the children are in the back and the driver is up front, be sure to ask the children if they are comfortable.

Drivers transporting children to school need to be aware of the school traffic rules for drop-off, pick-up, and parking and to obey them. If no one from the preschool child's class is there to meet the parent, she must park and accompany the child to her room.

Buses that transport preschool children need to be a part of the class's safety activities during the first week of school. You and the bus driver should provide a hands-on opportunity for all of the children to explore a school bus. Drivers need to explain how children should sit in the seats when the bus is moving. Buses that use seat belts can have children demonstrate their use. Drivers can explain how they learn their routes and let children out at the proper stop. The driver or transportation assistant can then show how children should climb down the bus stairs single file, holding onto the railing, wait at the bottom of the stairs for an adult to take their hand, and then proceed around the bus (and sometimes across the street) to a waiting adult; then practice going through the opposite routine for bus pick-up and loading. They also need to learn that they must stay in a safety zone of 10 feet away from all sides of the bus and never go behind it. Because preschool children are accompanied on and off the buses, the parent or assistant needs to know these rules as well.

Bus safety can be practiced in the classroom to great advantage. Children enjoy pretending to ride on a bus. Some classes have dramatic play equipment that includes a school bus, or you can make your own with rows of children's chairs for seats and a steering wheel toy for the driver. Use real seat belts if you have them. Provide bus driver hats, police hats, and stop signs. You might read one of the following books with a bus theme to get the children started.

Books with a Bus Theme

School Bus (Crews, 1984)

Every page of this simple, nearly wordless picture book is full of yellow school buses. A few of the pages have a brief line of text at the bottom saying such things as "empty yellow buses cross the town." They stop at red lights, go at green lights, pick up children, and finally drop them off at school. Then the reverse process takes place at the end of the day as the empty yellow buses fill up with children, carry them across town, and drop them off at their stops. Although the children look older than preschoolers, your youngsters will enjoy following these buses on their routes. Can they make up names for some of the children and tell stories about them riding the bus to school?

The Wheels on the Bus (Kovalski, 1987)

Here is the traditional song that most of the children already know in a picture book format. Joanna and Jenny go shopping with Grandma in London and sing the song while they are waiting for the red double-decker bus at the bus stop. But they get so carried away with the wipers on the bus going swish, swish, swish, the people on the bus hopping on and off, and the babies on the bus going waaa, waaa, waaa that when the bus finally comes—they miss it. Have the children sing the song as you read it. If you don't have the book, sing the song anyway and have children make up new words. How is this bus different from a school bus?

Me First (Lester, 1992)

Pinkerton, the protagonist of this story is a pink, plump, and pushy little pig who has to be the first in everything he does. He cuts ahead of the other kids and goes down the slide first. So of course when Pinkerton's Scout troop goes to the beach for a picnic in the school bus, he pushes everyone aside to get on the bus first and sit in the front row. Later he learns his lesson when someone calls, "Who would care for a sandwich?" and it turns out to be a little green witch living in the sand who makes Pinkerton care for her because he gets there first. Talk with your children about Pinkerton's playground and bus manners. Some bus manners your children may need to learn include those listed in Figure 3.3. Or have them decide on their own bus manners.

FIGURE 3.3

Bus Manners

- When bus is moving, sit, don't stand.
- Keep arms and hands out of windows.
- Keep bus aisles clear.
- Keep noise down so driver can hear.
- Walk single file without pushing when getting on and off bus.
- When dropping something near bus, wait till bus has gone to retrieve it.
- Walk only in front of bus holding a hand.

FIELD TRIPS

Making Field Trips Safe

Taking the children to visit interesting sites away from the classroom is an important part of any curriculum. If the sites are nearby the children may be able to walk. More distant sites may call for school bus trips. Insurance regulations usually rule out parents carrying children in their own cars. Parents and volunteers can help by accompanying the class and assisting teachers in keeping the children safe and accounted for.

Whether they walk or ride children should pair up in a buddy system with partners who will hold their hands while walking and sit on the bus next to them. Once at the site the buddies still need to keep track of one another. Young children tend to wander off, especially in new and strange surroundings.

Because all field trips involve safety issues for young children, it is important that you find out ahead of time as much as possible about the transportation to and from the site, what will occur at the site, and what safety hazards you may have to deal with.

Visiting the Site Ahead of Time

It is important for the teacher to check out the field trip site ahead of time, looking for possible safety problems, as well as anticipating what inappropriate behavior the children might pursue. Personnel at the site may not be aware of the short attention spans of children ages three, four, and five, or the endless curiosity they exhibit.

On your visit to the site find out what type of information the children will be getting and how this will happen. Will a resource person lecture to them? Will someone guide them around the site, explaining what they are looking at and answering questions? Will they have to stand in one spot for a long time? Will they be allowed to get close to things, touch things, and climb up on things? Will they be free to ask questions? Will they be free to investigate things on their own?

Talk with the resource person at the site alerting him or her to the nature of young children. Arrange for small groups of children at a time to go through the site. Try to make sure the information is age-appropriate. Try to discourage long lectures. If hands-on experiences are possible, make sure they are safe for young children. Do special arrangements need to be made for special needs children? Also find out how long the children will be staying at the site. As Redleaf (1983) suggests:

> Notice the physical setup (where the bus should stop or you should park,
> what door to come in, bathroom locations, and good places for regrouping
> or snacking.) The more familiar you are with the site, the more you can
> help make the introduction and on-site comments suitable for your group. (p. 189)

Be sure to note any safety features you may need to deal with. Will there be any machinery, open water, moving vehicles, or other dangers for the children? Will you be able to monitor the children at all times?

Dramatizing the Process of Going on the Trip

After you have talked to the children about the trip you are going to take, shown them pictures, and read them stories, it helps to have them dramatize the process of going on the actual trip. In a practice run like this children can learn what is expected of them, and you as the teacher can learn what you can expect from the children. Because everything will be new and different for the youngsters, they may react in unexpected ways. A run-through will help you and the children to establish the necessary field trip manners.

You can take a small group at a time on a pretend trip around the classroom. Have them hold their buddies' hands, go up the steps of the pretend bus, sit next to their buddy on the bus, look out the window and make comments of what they see, get off the bus, walk over to the site, and go through it. You can pretend to be the bus driver and then the resource person at the site, making comments on what you see and what they should look for. Besides making the process a more meaningful one for the children, a practice trip also helps to reduce any anxiety they may feel about going to an unknown setting. If they become separated, have them tell someone at the site.

It is best not to take trips too far during the first few weeks of school. Some children may still not be acclimated to the classroom, and a distant trip may be frightening. If you have visited the site, say, a farm, and realize that children unfamiliar with farm animals may become frightened of the noises they make, you can do as Redleaf suggests and dramatize this aspect of the trip in advance.

69

"Some animals make loud noises. Let's all oink as loud as we can to see what it might be like at the farm." Although it is not possible to guess ahead of time what may prove frightening to a particular child, it is worthwhile to identify some potentially frightening aspects and think of ways to prepare the children for them. (p. 190)

Using Parents and Volunteers

It is important that several parents or other volunteers accompany the class. Each one can be assigned to a small group of children or to a single child who may need special help. If you know a particular child frightens easily, you might ask a volunteer to stay close to the child, hold her hand, and try to help her overcome her fright.

Be sure to talk with parents and volunteers ahead of time telling them what has been planned, what they can expect, and what their role will be. If some have brought cameras or camcorders, encourage them to take pictures but at the same time keep an eye on the children they have been assigned to. Tell them what the limits are on child behavior and how to remind children to practice the manners they have learned. If children get out of hand you can take over.

Field Trip Manners

Children already know about bus manners (see Figure 3.3). They can be reminded about practicing bus manners as they ride to the field trip. If they are on a walking field trip they need to practice the street manners they have learned (see Figure 3.2). You should be the one to establish firmly the rule of children holding hands with their buddy and walking with the group, not running ahead. Take the children outside to practice their walking manners every time you go on a field trip. Afterwards express your appreciation of the way they walked together and stayed together. But if anyone runs ahead of the group, stop the walk, remind the children again of staying together, and try it again. It is helpful if one adult stays at the head of the group, and one at the rear. If they need to cross a street the lead adult can go ahead when traffic has stopped and the children can follow two at a time behind one another holding hands with their buddy. Figure 3.4 shows field trip manners children should follow.

FIGURE 3.4

Field Trip Manners

- Hold your buddy's hand as you walk.
- Stay with the group, don't run ahead.
- Sit in the bus next to your buddy.
- Keep track of your buddy at the site.
- Listen to the teacher or parent volunteer.
- If you become frightened go to the teacher or volunteer.
- If you become separated go to someone at the site and tell them.

Field Trip Sites for Preschool Children

The sites listed below are examples of field trip sites young children have taken either by bus or walking if the site was nearby. Look over your own neighborhood for other ideas.

Airport	Construction Site	Gas Station	Museum	Plant Nursery
Aquarium	Doctor's Office	Greenhouse	Music Store	Post Office
Bakery	Farm	Hairdresser	New House	Zoo
Bookstore	Fire Station	Hospital	Park	
Bowling Alley	Flea Market	Laundromat	Pet Shop	
Business Office	Florist	Library	Photo Store	
Car Repair	Garden	Monument	Pizza Restaurant	

Follow-Up Safety Activities

Once back in the classroom the children will be engaged in many follow-up activities such as drawing pictures of the trip, building block structures they saw on the trip, telling stories about the trip, singing songs about the trip, enacting dramatic play scenarios about the trip, or dictating stories about the photos that were taken. This is the time to insert reminders of the good safety manners they exhibited. If you can find a picture book about the site you visited, you might read it to individuals and small groups, asking them to look for the safety manners they practiced.

My Visit to the Aquarium (Aliki, 1993)

This book makes a perfect follow-up to the visit a class may take to a large aquarium. It is the first-person story of a boy, his little sister, and his big brother as they wander through the wonderful world of sea life in a large aquarium. Children of all ages are shown looking at the marine exhibits, holding hands with each other or their parents as they walk along. Children of every ethnic group, as well as one on crutches and one in a wheelchair exclaim over the sights of gorgeous coral fish, waddling penguins, a giant kelp forest, sharks and barracudas. Only one child seems to be running and two are leaning rather far over the bat ray pool. Do your children pick them out as not practicing safety manners? Books such as this one can often be purchased in gift shops located in museums, and help children to recapture and understand the field trip adventure they have just completed.

THIS CHAPTER'S ROLE

Safety, the Outdoor Curriculum promotes playground safety by describing how to set up playground equipment to make a safe environment; how to educate children through playground manners to use the equipment safely; how the classroom staff can carry out playground supervision and work with children to create rules that can be enforced consistently. A Playground Safety Checklist helps teachers to inspect the playground and maintain safety on a daily basis. Street safety for preschool children describes pedestrian rules for crossing the street as children walk to school or on field trips. Transportation safety describes seat belt and car safety as well as rules for bus safety. Making field trips safe includes visiting the site ahead of time by the teacher, dramatizing the process of going on a field trip by the children, using parents and volunteers to accompany the trips, and teaching children to follow field trip manners. Books with outdoor safety themes are described along with ideas for children to put safety manners into practice.

WHAT HAVE YOU LEARNED FROM THIS CHAPTER?

1. What is the most common slide injury for preschool children and how can you reduce it?

2. What makes the platform at the top of a slide safe?

3. Why is the "fall zone" around swings so much larger than other equipment fall zones?

4. What are "trapping hazards" on climbing equipment and how can you reduce them?

5. How is children's play at outside sand and water tables different from play at inside sand and water tables?

6. What kind of playground equipment is not recommended for preschoolers? Why?

7. How do you get children to act safely on the playground without harsh threats?

8. If you were a playground supervisor when would you bring children inside? Why?

9. What kinds of pedestrian safety do city children younger than 10 years old need to learn?

10. Before taking preschool children on a field trip what should you do to make it safe?

HOW CAN YOU APPLY WHAT YOU HAVE LEARNED?

1. Use the Playground Safety Checklist to check on safety features in your program's playground. What changes do you need to make?

2. Describe the piece of playground equipment you would purchase for your playground and tell why you chose this particular piece.

3. Describe the "Create-a-Playground" you would erect if you did not have any playground equipment.

4. Read one of the books with a playground theme to your children and discuss the playground manners they would use in the story. How do they respond?

5. What playground manners would you want to enforce on your playground and how would you do it?

6. Walk with a preschool child over to a crosswalk and demonstrate the pedestrian safety rules he or she should use. Describe what happens.

7. Read one of the books with a pedestrian safety theme to your children. Then take them on a pretend classroom walk around such a city and ask them what they would do at each stop you make.

8. Bring a car seat belt to class and set up a pretend car with chairs as car seats and a steering wheel in front. Can they demonstrate the proper use of the seat belt?

9. Have children make a list of bus manners they should be using. How is it the same or different from the list in Figure 3.3?

10. Take a group of preschool children on a pretend classroom field trip to a fire station, following the guidelines in Figure 3.4, Field Trip Manners. What happens?

REFERENCES

American Academy of Pediatrics. (2002). *Caring for our children.* Elk Grove Village, IL: Author.

Flynn, L. L., & Kieff, J. (2002). Including everyone in outdoor play. *Young Children, 57*(3), 20–26.

Griffin, C., & Rinn, B. (1998). Enhancing outdoor play with an obstacle course. *Young Children, 53*(3), 18–23.

Owen, M., & Patterson, C. (2001). Potential for partnership: Early childhood road safety education at home and preschool. *Australian Journal of Early Education, 26*(3), 38.

Readdick, C. A., & Park, J. J. (1998). Achieving great heights: The climbing child. *Young Children, 53*(6), 14–19.

Redleaf, R. (1983). *Open the door let's explore: Neighborhood field trips for young children.* Minneapolis, MN: Redleaf Press.

Settle, M. B., & Price, S.C. (2002). *Complete Idiot's Guide to Child Safety.* Indianapolis, IN: Macmillan USA.

Stephenson, A. (2002). What George taught me about toddlers and water. *Young Children, 57*(3), 10–14.

Stoll, B. H. (2000). *A to Z health and safety in the child care setting*. St. Paul, MN: Redleaf Press.

United States Consumer Product Commission. (1997). *Handbook for public playground safety*. Washington, D.C.: Author.

SUGGESTED READINGS

American Society for Testing and Materials. (1998). *Standard consumer safety performance specifications for playground equipment for public use*. West Conshohocken, PA: Author.

DeBord, K., Hestenes, L. L., Moore, R. C., Cosco, N., & McGinnis, J.R. (2002). Paying attention to the outdoor environment is as important as preparing the indoor environment. *Young Children, 57*(3), 32–35.

Frost, J. L., & Sutterby, J. A. (2002). Making playgrounds fit for children and children fit on playgrounds. *Young Children, 57*(3), 36–41.

Frost, J. L., & Sweeney, T. B. (1996). *Cause and prevention of playground injuries and litigation*. Olney, MD: Association for Childhood Education International.

Helm, J. H., & Katz, L. (2001). *Young investigators: The project approach in the early years*. New York: Teachers College Press.

Hennniger, M. (1994). Planning for outdoor play. *Young Children, 49*(4), 10–15.

Hearron, P. F., & Hildebrand, V. (2003). *Management of child development centers* (5th ed.). Upper Saddle River, NJ: Merrill/Prentice Hall.

Hudson, S., Mack, J., & Thompson, D. (2000). *How safe are America's playgrounds? A national profile of children, school, and park playgrounds*. Cedar Falls, IA: National Program for Playground Safety.

Owens, K. (1997). The developmentally appropriate designed playground. In S. Hudson & D. Thompson (Eds.), *The SAFE playground handbook* (pp. 51–60). Cedar Falls, IA: National Program for Playground Safety.

CHILDREN'S BOOKS

Aliki. (1993). *My visit to the aquarium.* New York: HarperCollins.

Best, C. (1995). *Red light, green light, Mama and me.* New York: Orchard Books.

Crews, D. (1984). *School bus.* New York: Mulberry.

Dillon, L., & Dillon, D. (2002). *Rap a tap tap: Here's Bojangles—Think of that!* New York: Blue Sky Press.

Gorbachev, V. (2001). *Chicken chickens.* New York: North-South Books.

Kovalski, M. (1987). *The wheels on the bus.* Boston: Little, Brown and Co.

Lester. H. (1992). *Me first.* Boston: Houghton Mifflin.

Mennen, I., & Daly, N. (1990). *Somewhere in Africa.* New York: Dutton.

Mitton, T. (2001). *Down by the cool of the pool.* New York: Orchard Books.

Shannon, D. (2002). *Duck on the bike.* New York: Blue Sky Press.

Chapter 4

EMERGENCY PREPAREDNESS

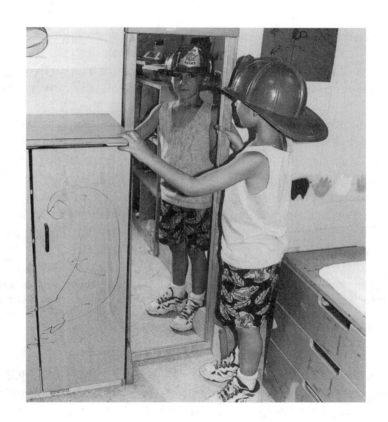

**CATASTROPHIC EVENTS
ACCIDENTS
FIRE EMERGENCIES
WEATHER EMERGENCIES
NATURAL DISASTERS**

CATASTROPHIC EVENTS

Child care professionals have always prided themselves on being prepared for any eventuality. When you work with young children you can never be sure what will happen next. As a result, you try to remain calm, open, and ready for anything. But after the surprise terrorist attacks of September 11, 2001, most of us have come to realize you can never really be prepared. However, there are steps you can take to protect your children and yourselves.

Remember the ideas discussed in Chapter 1? How you need to strengthen your inner core? Like putting on your oxygen mask first in a plane, you can help yourself first and then be ready to help the children by accepting yourself, appreciating yourself, and having compassion for others. That is your deep core of unconditional love. Helping children strengthen their own deep core is also significant but does not happen overnight. You and they need to work on these important aspects of strengthening yourselves over time.

Reducing Fear

No matter how strong you or they become, there is another feature of catastrophic events that you must deal with: fear. Fear in the face of danger can cause almost as much damage to people as the event itself. As a teacher of young children, you must find a way to overcome your own fear so that you remain a calm model for them to see. They look to you to see how you respond to such events as shootings, bombings, and explosions. If you fall apart, many of them will too. As Farish (2001) tells us:

> Helping young children deal with their feelings and thoughts is especially
> challenging when we adults haven't had time to deal with our own reactions;
> when we are grieving, afraid, and angry...we should remember that even
> very young children notice a great deal and they can quickly tune into any
> sorrow or anxiety that surrounds them. (p. 6)

Make yourself familiar with Figure 1.7 in Chapter 1, Strategies for Helping Children Lessen Fears. These seven suggestions can play an important role in keeping both you and the children calm in the face of danger. When you yourself are involved in helping others, your children, you will have little time to think of yourself.

The first strategy asks you to "remove or reduce the cause of fear if possible." In the case of a community disturbance you may need to keep the children where they are for the time being. You may want to bring the children together. Have them sit on the floor in a circle where you can speak quietly about what is happening. Do not turn on the television if you should have one, but talk calmly to them in simple terms that they will understand. Tell them that you will take care of them, no matter what, and that they will be all right. If any of them have questions or comments, let them express themselves, but answer them in a positive manner. Then sing a happy song just as you usually do to conclude circle time.

Continue with your familiar classroom activities: free choice, cleanup, snack, story time, lunch, and naptime. Following the ordinary schedule helps children feel that all is well in the classroom. You may need to skip the outdoor playground time just as you do on rainy days. If emergency vehicles are roaring by, lights flashing and sirens screaming, you may want to pull the curtains closed so children are not running to the windows or becoming alarmed all over again. Instead, this may be the time for reading a book about emergencies to help children understand what is happening.

Book with Emergency Theme

Emergency! (Mayo, 2002)

This book features emergency vehicles such as a police car, an ambulance, a rescue crane, a marine rescue boat, a police motorcycle, a forest fire fighting plane, a snow plow, a fire truck, a rescue helicopter, and a tow truck. Each double page shows the vehicle speeding to the rescue with the last words stating: "Help is coming. It's on it's way." The last page shows a quiet community with all of the emergency vehicles parked in garages, ready and waiting for the next 911 call. Then, as the book tells the reader, help will be coming to save the day.

If you decide to read this book because of the emergency vehicles going by the school, do it in a calm manner, not excitedly. If children have questions, answer them matter-of-factly. Then get out the toy emergency vehicles for play in the block center or sand table. It is no use to hide what is happening from young children. But you can reduce their confusion and fear by reading, talking about, and acting out certain aspects of the situation. As Farish notes:

> When children witness violent events and the consequences that follow,
> either firsthand or on television, the result is often fear and confusion.
> Young children are most fearful when they do not understand what is
> happening around them. (p. 6)

This book, of course, is one that can be read ahead of time, before an emergency occurs, and when the situation is calmer. Then it can be repeated any time an emergency vehicle zooms by the school. Some nervous children may always be alarmed, but if you can help them understand that such vehicles are hurrying off to help people, they may find themselves becoming calmer during emergencies. Ask the children why emergency vehicles sound sirens. We assume that children already know, but they do not until it is explained to them. It is important to have little toy vehicles like this for children to play with at any time.

Individual Attention

Some children need your individual attention when catastrophic events occur. As Figure 1.7 suggests: "Allow child to cry." There is nothing wrong with tears, you may remember. They are a means for releasing the chemical toxins that are built up during stress. You may want to cry yourself, but you need to save your tears until later when you are away from the children. Let individual children know that feeling upset like this is okay. But once crying children have stopped, try to get them involved in calming activities. Water play with basters, squeeze bottles, pouring implements, and egg beaters in the water table can help to relieve emotional stress in many children. Others may prefer finger painting where they can swish different colors of paint around as much as they want. Give them large sheets of butcher paper on a table and encourage them to move their fingers, hands, and even arms as they work off their feelings.

Some may want to talk about the event. Encourage each one to express how they feel. Give them some words to use to get them started. "Do you feel sort of shaky, Alonzo? Can you tell me what it feels like inside of you?" Others may want to sit at a table and put their heads down. You can have them close their eyes and think of something beautiful or their favorite color if they want to.

Emergency Evacuation

You can be prepared ahead of time if you know that emergency evacuations may be called for. Your center director or school principal needs to arrange for and designate a primary and secondary evacuation site. You will need to prepare and have on hand at all times an emergency duffel bag. The bag should contain as follows:

FIGURE 4.1

Contents of Emergency Duffel Bag

1. Bottled water
2. Paper cups
3. Snacks (crackers, dried fruit)
4. Battery operated radio and extra batteries
5. A blanket
6. First aid supplies and first aid handbook
7. Emergency contact information for each child and employee
8. Cell phone
9. Cards with games and songs

This bag should be clearly marked and not too heavy so that it can be carried easily by a staff member during an evacuation. The contact information needs to include both home and work numbers for parents or persons authorized to pick up the child. It is also suggested that you have an out-of-town contact number as well as a photo of each child. (Terrass, M. Z., 2002)

Center directors and teaching staff need to formulate an emergency evacuation plan ahead of time which they should communicate to appropriate personnel at the evacuation sites, as well as to parents at the time they enroll their children, and whenever they change to a new site. You need to practice this plan with the children and evacuation site personnel on a regular basis. Children can learn "evacuation manners" just as they learned field trip manners.

Keeping Children Calm at an Evacuation Site

Once children have been safely assembled at an evacuation site, you will need to involve them in quiet activities to keep them occupied, and to keep their minds off the event that has transpired. Many teachers carry cards with them with the words of songs, fingerplays, or descriptions of various simple games they might play with the children.

Guessing games: 1) "I'm thinking of something (e.g., blue) that someone is wearing. What is it? 2) Guess how many fingers I have held up behind my back. 3) Close your eyes and guess who I am going to tap on the head. 4) Guess what I have in my pocket. 5) Guess what I have in the duffel bag that is good to eat.

When someone guesses the answer to one of these games, let that person keep the game going by taking a turn as the questioner. When someone guesses the answer to game #5, he or she can distribute one of the snacks.

Fingerplays: *Eentsy Weentsy Spider; Teddy Bear Teddy Bear Turn Around; The Lady with the Alligator Purse; Silly Sally Went to Town; We're Going on a Bear Hunt*

Songs: *This Old Man; The Wheels on the Bus; Where Is Thumbkin; If You're Happy and You Know it; Miss Mary Mack; John Jacob Jingleheimer Schmidt*

Post Traumatic Stress Disorder

Children experiencing this disorder have been exposed to an extreme traumatic event that involves actual or threatened death or serious injury to themselves, or the witnessing of an event that involves violent death, serious harm or injury to someone close to them that is outside a child's life experiences. It is a psychological response to a severe emotional experience. While most young children come through catastrophic tragedies with few persistent effects, a few children do suffer Post Traumatic Stress Disorder (PTSD).

Because teachers have been in close contact with the children prior to the traumatic event, they are in a unique position to note any changes or aftereffects in a child's behavior. Characteristic symptoms of PTSD include:

FIGURE 4.2

Some Symptoms of Children's Post Traumatic Stress Disorder

- Increased separation anxiety with parents
- Clinging behavior with adults
- Changes in eating and sleeping habits
- Frequent crying spells
- Avoidance of reminders of the event
- Re-experiencing the event (flashbacks)
- Thought pattern interruptions focusing on event
- Persistent play themes related to event
- Rebellious and aggressive behaviors
- Thumb-sucking and bed-wetting
- Fewer interactions with other children

[Adapted from Grosse, S. J. (2001) and Celitti, A. (2002)]

A number of the children may temporarily exhibit some of these symptoms directly after the traumatic event. But if many of a child's symptoms persist for more than a month, teachers should suggest that parents talk to a professional about it. In the meantime, you should be involved with helping all of the children to recover from the trauma. First, they need to have an informal "debriefing" with you about what has happened and how they feel about it. You can talk with small groups or the total group. Some may not yet be up to talking about the event. Do not force them. For those who do wish to talk, you should be an active listener, waiting patiently for them to have their say, then following up with supportive comments. Vacca (2001) cautions teachers to proceed slowly, following the children's lead, and to be sure rapport is established first. He believes that:

> Look, listen, and feel are the three elements to help children deal
> with a traumatic event. Throughout this process, children come to
> understand and learn appropriate ways to express a variety of
> feelings. (p. 23)

Next, children need to return to the normal routines of the program. Again, some may not be ready. Do not force them. Children need to regain a sense of trust in their immediate environment. On the other hand, they may be ready to hear a humorous tale or two about animals with problems of their own to solve.

Books with a Humorous Problem-Solving Theme

My Truck Is Stuck! (Lewis, K & Kirk, D., 2002)

A dog is driving a big red dump truck piled high with doggy bones across the desert when suddenly one of its wheels plunges into a large prairie dog hole. As other vehicles full of animal travelers proceed down the road, the dog hops out, waving a sign saying "Help! Please Help!" Everyone driving along tries to help by tying their vehicles one by one to the truck or the next vehicle in line and pulling, but the truck doesn't budge. Large colorful two-page illustrations accompanied by funny verses try to keep this procession moving along, but without success. A car full of travelers, a van with a moving man, a very steep jeep, a school bus (what a fuss), all pull, but still nothing works. Finally a tow truck with a mechanic (don't panic) lifts up the truck and pulls it out. But there is something else at work here. Do your listeners notice it in the pictures? The prairie dogs who started the whole affair have taken all the bones one by one out of the back of the truck until it is empty! What do your listeners think if that?

You should be prepared to extend this story by providing your listeners with doggy bones (Styrofoam "peanuts" or golf tees) for one of their toy dump trucks, some pipe cleaners for rope to tie other vehicles together, and turn the children loose to enact their own stuck truck dilemma. Might this story finally brighten their day?

Cuckoo Can't Find You (Siomades, 2002)

The cuckoo bird asks readers to help the different animals in this book find the items that they are looking for. This is a book for one or two listeners seated on either side of the reader. It will take sharp eyes for them to pick out the objects hidden somewhere on each page. For instance, the bear's pear is hidden in its leg. Even you may not be able to find the items at first glance! Where is that stork's fork? But it is the last page that children can't wait for. Cuckoo can't find you! And there is a round silver mirror to find yourself in.

Have the original listeners invite other children to try to find the items as they flip through the book. Another day you can bring in some of the items and hide them one by one around the classroom. The child who finds the first item gets to hide the next one in this game. Does this activity take the children's minds off the trauma they have experienced?

Children who have been traumatized need to regain control of themselves and their environment again. Some may regain their sense of self through laughter or story re-enactments like this. Others may use puppets, dramatic play, or art to release their emotional upheaval. You will need to provide many experiences for children to release tension and cope with their feelings. Give them time for therapeutic experiences with painting, clay, play dough, water, and sand. Have them dictate stories. Children three and four years old are not too young to be aware of big and terrible events. They need to be able to talk about them with the adults in their lives. They need to be able to get in touch with their feelings through painting or modeling with clay or acting out the event. As Gross and Clemens (2002) point out:

> Rather than banning play or art containing violence, adults should
> help children use these activities to work out an understanding,
> regain control, and reach some resolution on the violence they see. (p. 47)

When four-year-old Emma painted a picture of the New York fire resulting from the Twin Towers collapse, she splashed red paint up and down on her paper and then clawed through it with her fingers. She told her teacher that the red fire she had painted was torn because that's what happened to the towers. This prompted other children to paint their versions of the tragedy and talk about it. The teacher was so impressed that children this young were able to express and discuss such a painful event, that she changed her whole view of young children.

> I'm learning to revise my image of the child. For many years I've been
> working on seeing the child as full, rich in experience, not as empty and
> waiting for adults to fill him or her up. When Emma spoke so directly of
> her desire to know about the towers and the fighting, I experienced her
> not as a helpless little child, but as a powerful human being. (Gross &
> Clemens, p. 49)

Figure 4.3 lists some strategies teachers can use to help children recover from trauma.

FIGURE 4.3

Strategies for Helping Children Cope with Trauma

- Talk with children about what happened.
- Proceed slowly, be an active listener.
- Assure children they are safe in classroom.
- Help children get involved in normal classroom routines.
- Read and discuss appropriate stories.
- Encourage children to act out the traumatic event.
- Set up painting, clay, play dough, water, and sand activities.
- Provide appropriate follow-up.

ACCIDENTS

Teachers of preschool children can prepare for accidents in several ways. First you should post near the telephone and with any cell phones the emergency numbers for police, sheriff, fire department, doctor, ambulance, hospital, and poison control center. All adults in the classroom should be familiar with the location of these numbers. Also, post near telephones simple directions for handling emergencies. If your program is bilingual, be sure to write these directions in two languages. Another list of telephone numbers posted near the phones should be the children's home phone numbers, parents' cell phone numbers, and numbers of persons to contact if no one is home.

Emergencies in which quick action is required and in which you should call 911, the Emergency Medical Services number, include:

- Lack of breathing
- Severe bleeding
- Shock, fainting, heatstroke
- Chemical eye injuries
- Clothing on fire
- Choking
- Drowning

You or someone on your staff should be trained to give first aid for any of these emergencies. It is essential that at least one and preferably all of the teaching staff be trained in first aid, CPR, and Heimlich choke procedures.

In addition, be sure to keep an easy-to-use, easy-to-read first-aid emergency handbook near the emergency numbers. A spiral-bound tabbed guide with basic information on separate colored flaps is *Childhood Emergencies: What to do,* (Marin Child Care Council, 2000). Another spiral-bound book with logs, forms, procedures, and fact sheets, as well as individual child care plans is *A to Z Health and Safety in the Child Care Setting,* (Stoll, 2000).

Two first aid kits are necessary in each classroom: one for the room and one for taking on field trips. All of the classroom staff should be familiar with the contents and know how to use them. Figure 4.4 lists the contents of a first-aid kit.

FIGURE 4.4

First-Aid Kit Contents

1. Scissors	11. Disposable gloves
2. Tweezers	12. Antiseptic or alcohol wipes
3. Thermometer	13. Pen/pencil and notepad
4. Bandage tape	14. Syrup of ipecac
5. Sterile gauze pads	15. Coins for use in pay phone
6. Flexible roller gauze	16. Insect sting preparation
7. Triangular bandages	17. Water
8. Safety pins	18. Small plastic splints
9. Eye dressing	19. Soap
10. Emergency telephone numbers	

[Adapted from American Academy of Pediatrics (2002)]

Accidents can happen anywhere at any time. As a teacher of young children you are already becoming adept at anticipating ahead of time what children might do. This skill should help you prevent most accidents in the classroom, on the playground, and on field trips. Should accidents happen to children, it will depend upon the kind and severity of the accident as to the action you will take. With at least two staff members available at all times, one can calm the child and apply first aid measures such as stopping bleeding, and bandaging cuts, while the other staff member makes any necessary calls (e.g., to a parent, to an emergency number). The other children can be directed to continue with their activities.

As you attend the injured child, remain calm and help the child to calm down, tell her help is on the way and you will stay with her. Let her cry if she needs to, but speak in soothing tones and help to redirect her away from her injury. Children can become aware of situations requiring first aid before an accident happens, by having stories read about helping someone who has been injured. When a real injury does occur, be sure to write down what happened and when, the child's reaction, and your own response. Put such information on your program's accident report form with copies to be passed along to parents and emergency personnel.

Book with a First Aid Theme

Maybe a Band-Aid Will Help (Hines, 1984)

When Sarah's doll Abigail lost her leg, Sarah tried to get her mother to fix her right away. But mother was busy doing one thing after another, so Sarah tried to fix her herself. The band-aid didn't work, so Sarah tried sewing the leg on but ended up pricking her own finger. At last mother took time and the three of them played hospital in which Abigail's leg was finally sewn back on.

Your children can carry out their own pretend first aid experiences in the dramatic play center with hospital and doctor props, and some real band-aids for the injured dolls. Such play is not only therapeutic for children who might be frightened in the face of real injuries, but also helpful for teachers to learn what children know about injuries and first aid.

FIRE EMERGENCIES

The best preparedness for a fire emergency is preventing a fire from happening in the first place. All schools and child care facilities should have regular inspections of their buildings regarding fire walls, panic bars on doors, removal of harmful materials, two exits from every location, smoke alarms, and fire extinguishers strategically placed.

Electric and gas utilities can inspect their equipment to make sure it is properly installed and maintained. Too many fires start in faulty electrical equipment. (Hendricks, 2002). Local fire departments can provide fire safety training for staff. Kitchen staff especially should learn that combustible materials must be stored away from heat sources. They should also learn how to put out skillet fires with baking soda and tight-fitting lids, as well as using a fire extinguisher. If a kitchen fire should start they need to know how to first sound the alarm and then get all the children out of the building. Hendricks recommends the following:

- Properly place and maintain smoke detectors.
- Make sure staff knows two ways out from every part of building.
- Post floor plan showing quickest route out of building.
- Maintain clear exit paths through halls and stairwells.
- Install emergency lighting.
- Be sure all exit doors are unlocked from the inside and outside.
- Keep emergency duffel bag near classroom exit.

Because young children's thin skin burns more easily than adults' and children's quick breathing takes in smoke more rapidly, it is imperative that you prepare for exiting in a fire emergency with carefully thought out plans and frequent practice drills. No matter how many false alarms you may experience (even in one day), the next one may be the real thing, so treat them all seriously. Fire drills, earthquake drills, chemical spills, and explosions call for buildings to be cleared as quickly as possible. Children and staff members should practice this procedure repeatedly so that everyone understands how to do it without panic. Do not wait for a fire inspector to make this happen. It is your responsibility to yourself, the children, and their families to see that emergency evacuations are accomplished with ease. Whenever a smoke alarm goes off treat it as a real fire and evacuate.

You need to practice exiting from alternate escape routes in case there is smoke in a hall. If this is the case someone needs to hold up a sign in the hall saying: "No Exit— Smoke in Hall." Then your line of children needs to practice reversing itself and going in the opposite direction with your end-of-line staff member now in the lead. Be sure your practices include the sounding of the real fire alarm so that children will learn to carry on in spite of the ear-splitting noise. Emergency exiting demands rules and order. You can help children follow the rules by practicing them calmly but consistently over and over, so no straggling or out-of-control behavior occurs. Time it with a stop watch. Children enjoy keeping track like this. Figure 4.5 lists actions to take during a fire emergency exiting.

FIGURE 4.5

Rules for Emergency Exiting of Building
1. Line up children quickly but calmly.
2. Teacher at head of line, staff member at rear.
3. Teacher carry emergency duffel bag and daily attendance sheet.
4. Follow quickest safe route to outside.
5. Assemble at evacuation site outside building.
6. Count to make sure all children are there.

Children with physical impairments may need special help exiting the building. A staff member can be assigned to children with special needs to help them move quickly and safely out of the building. Be sure the program is in handicap compliance, with exit ramps, railings, and handholds in place. Designate a safe site outside the building where all children should assemble whenever there is emergency exiting.

If you or a staff member is called upon to operate a fire extinguisher before you exit the building be sure you understand what to do. The procedure written in easily read directions should be posted next to the extinguisher, telling the operator to:

1. Hold Upright, Pull Pin
2. Point Nozzle to Base of Fire
3. Squeeze Trigger and Sweep Side-to-Side

(Stoll, 2002, p. 39)

In the event of a real fire, you may need to put into operation your Strategies for Helping Children Cope with Trauma, Figure 4.3. Once back in the classroom you can talk with the children about what has happened, assuring them that all of you are safe because you followed the rules you learned. Listen closely to what the children have to say. In the days to follow some children may want to work out their feelings in paint, clay, play dough, water or sand. Others may want to act out the event in the dramatic play center. This is the time to bring out firefighter hats, jackets, and boots. Have toy fire trucks and emergency vehicles in the block center and sand table. Read books with fire emergency themes.

Books with Fire Emergency Theme

Stop Drop and Roll (Cuyler, 2001)

Jessica worried about everything. When her teacher taught the class about fire safety, and what to do if their clothes caught on fire, poor Jessica worried so much she was sure she would never remember what to do. "Stop, slop, and troll," she muttered. She even made her family at home have a fire drill. But at Tom's birthday party when the candles were lit, she suddenly remembered and screamed out: "Stop, drop, and roll!" which sent Tom rolling under the table. A false alarm, but better to be safe than sorry.

The story is for somewhat older children but preschoolers can follow it easily, and should have interesting comments to make when you read it to a small group. Are they frightened like Jessica seems to be? What would they do?

Even Firefighters Hug Their Moms (Maclean, 2002)

In this book the boy main character calls himself Big Frank when he dresses up in his fire hat, boots, and protective gear. He wears a face mask to help him breathe when the pretend smoke is as thick as a milkshake. But he is too busy fighting fires with the vacuum cleaner hose to hug his mom. When he is Officer Dave, his little sister Sally is Rex, his police dog. Still no hug for mom. Then he is Joe the EMT, Emergency Medical Technician, driving an ambulance with a pan lid steering wheel, racing to the hospital with the siren on all the way. No time for hugs yet. When he is Rick, the garbage truck driver, he gets things back for a lady who has thrown out something by mistake. She is so happy she tries to give him a hug and he lets her, because even garbage truck drivers hug their moms.

Your boys may want to pretend to be these and other characters in the book, (e.g., doctor, construction worker, helicopter pilot, train conductor, and astronaut), but your girls may have trouble adapting to the secondary roles. Girls can be firefighters too, they will show you. Put out some of the props shown if any children want to play these roles. Children experiencing real trauma may treat this story more seriously than intended. It is also a good follow-up story for children's visits to a fire station or hospital.

WEATHER EMERGENCIES

Violent weather can cause emergencies in which teachers must be prepared to protect children. When warnings for tornadoes, tropical storms, hurricanes, typhoons, flash floods, tidal waves, windstorms, or dust storms are issued, or sirens are sounded, emergency procedures must be followed immediately. Different rules are necessary for different types of storms. Learn the rules that apply to your area, and practice them with the children under your care until they can respond quickly and without panic.

In electrical storms children need to come indoors as quickly as possible. If they are caught outside, they should not stand under tall trees or on hills. They should get out of water immediately and may need to wait out the storm in a vehicle. Inside the classroom computers and TVs should be unplugged and telephones disconnected. In tornadoes children should go to the lowest location in the building or get near inside walls, in hallways, and away from windows. In hurricanes and typhoons children may need to be evacuated to an emergency shelter if there is no time for parents to pick them up. Parents should be informed of all your emergency plans.

Once again it is fear that causes much of the turmoil in the classroom. No matter how dangerous the weather, if preparations are carried out in a calm manner with the teacher and other adults not showing signs of panic, the children are likely to remain calm themselves. Even if children have to hurry to get inside, once in the room they can slow down and calm down. Figure 1.7, Strategies for Helping Children Lessen Fears in Chapter 1 gives suggestions you can follow to help children relax and remain unruffled. You may also want to read a book with a weather theme so children see how the characters behave in the face of dangerous weather.

Books with a Dangerous Weather Theme

Storm Is Coming! (Tekavec, 2002)

In this farmyard story the farmer warns that "storm" is coming and all the animals must hurry inside the barn. Dog rounds up the sheep barking that storm is coming and they must get in the barn quickly, managing to frighten them badly. The sheep tell the duck; the duck tells the cows, and they all rush inside. Since they don't know what storm looks like, they choose duck as their lookout, and he sends down reports from an opening in the hayloft. He never sees storm, but he tells them about dark clouds that will hide storm, a big wind that will blow him away, a flashing in the sky that will blind him, and a growling in the clouds that is sure to frighten storm away. When the barn door creaks open, the animals huddle in the shadows knowing that storm is finally coming to get them. But it is only the farmer telling them it's safe to come out now.

Can your listeners tell you why the animals were so frightened? Whom did they think storm was? Is this another case of being afraid of the unknown? How do they feel about storm?

Aunt Minnie and the Twister (Prigger, 2002)

Here is another farm story but with children involved, lots of children. Aunt Minnie lives on a little farm in Kansas with her nine orphaned nieces and nephews. No matter how crowded her little house becomes, Minnie always says, "We don't have much room—but we have each other." When she wants their attention, she stands on the front porch, rings an old school bell, and the kids come running. One day the wind blew, the sky turned black and a funnel cloud started forming. She rang her bell, and told the kids to hold onto each other and run for the root cellar. They made it just in time, slamming the door behind them as hailstones cracked against it. When the tornado was over they all came out to see what mischief the twister had done. It had turned her little house completely around and they had to build a new room on the old front and a new front porch on the old back of the house, but they still had each other.

What do your listeners think about this large family and all of their goings-on? Is there anything those children are frightened of? What about the twister? What would your children have done in the face of the storm?

NATURAL DISASTERS

Natural disasters such as floods, earthquakes, and volcanic eruptions need to be treated by you and your staff in much the same way that you treat catastrophic events: reducing fear, being prepared with a plan for emergency evacuation, having an emergency duffle bag ready, and evacuating the children as soon as possible if this is appropriate. If there is ample warning, parents can pick up their own children, but in the event of an unexpected happening such as an earthquake, teachers may have other plans ready to put into operation. Children will need to evacuate a building as quickly as possible and gather at a designated safe site away from buildings. With volcanic eruptions, children should have already been evacuated if their building is too close. Otherwise, it is the ash in the air making breathing difficult that should keep children inside until parents are able to pick them up. Floods usually mean retreating to higher ground, but a flash flood poses a different problem. There may not be time to evacuate, thus children need to remain in one high spot in the building until rescued.

THIS CHAPTER'S ROLE

Chapter 4, Emergency Preparedness tells teachers and early childhood staff what to do in case of catastrophic events, by making yourself calm at first, then helping children to calm down by bringing them together and talking softly to them. Some children will need individual attention through calming activities, talking about how they feel, and allowing them to cry if necessary. Emergency evacuation is discussed, including how to assemble an emergency duffel bag that must be carried with you. Post traumatic stress disorder is described along with suggestions for helping children to recover. For using first aid in medical emergencies it is necessary for the staff to be trained in first aid, CPR, and Heimlich choke procedures. Fire emergencies may be prevented by having facilities inspected regularly. Fire emergency exiting for children and staff can be practiced until everyone is familiar with the routine. Preparation for weather emergencies involving tornadoes, severe electrical storms, or hurricanes is discussed, including how to reduce children's fears. Finally natural disasters such as floods, earthquakes, and volcanic eruptions are discussed, each needing its own plan to protect children.

WHAT HAVE YOU LEARNED FROM THIS CHAPTER?

1. How can you reduce your own and the children's fear in the face of catastrophic events?

2. What should you do if emergency vehicles rush by your building with sirens blaring?

3. How can you help an individual child to regain her composure after a catastrophic event?

4. How will you be able to tell if any of the children are suffering from post traumatic stress disorder after an event of this sort?

5. What can children do in the classroom to regain their sense of self after suffering from a trauma like this?

6. How can you be prepared for accidents in the preschool classroom or playground?

7. How can children be evacuated from the building in case of fire when one of the halls is filled with smoke?

8. Why is practice so important in preparing for a fire emergency? How can you carry it out?

9. What should you do if you are out on the playground with the children and an electrical storm begins?

10. What should you do in the event of an earthquake?

HOW CAN YOU APPLY WHAT YOU HAVE LEARNED?

1. Read and discuss a book with an emergency theme with the children. Then put out props in the dramatic play center or put emergency vehicles in the block center and have children enact what they would do.

2. Put together an Emergency Duffel Bag and explain how you would use each item in it.

3. Post emergency phone numbers near a phone in your classroom, along with a plan with directions for handling emergencies, and a floor plan showing two routes for classroom evacuation.

4. Assemble a first aid kit and describe how you would use each item in it.

5. Conduct two fire drills, one following the first evacuation route, and one in which the hall could be blocked with smoke. Describe the results.

6. Read and discuss a book with a fire emergency theme with the children. Then put out props in the dramatic play center and have children re-enact the story from the book.

7. How can you keep children calm at an evacuation site where they must remain for awhile? Describe several stories you might read or tell, fingerplays or game you could play or songs you could sing. Practice this with the children.

8. What would you do if you found that several children exhibited post traumatic stress disorder symptoms after a real fire and building evacuation?

9. What extension activities could you use with children after reading a book such as *My Truck Is Stuck*? (or another similar book). What would you expect them to learn from this?

10. Write up a safety plan for the children in case of a tornado or earthquake. Carry out a practice using this plan.

REFERENCES

Cellitti, A. (2002) Helping children cope with stress. Under *Keeping children safe and healthy.* http://www.earlychildhood.com/Articles/index.cfm?FuseAction-Article&A355.

Farish, J. M. (2001). Helping young children in frightening times. *Young Children, 56*(6), 6–7.

Gross, T., & Clemens, S. G. (2002). Painting a tragedy: Young children process the events of September 11. *Young Children, 57*(3), 44–51.

Grosse, S. J. (2001). Children and post traumatic stress disorder: What classroom teachers should know. *ERIC Digest,* ED460122.

Hendricks, C. (2002). Fire prevention in child care. http://www.earlychildhood.com/Articles/index.cfm?FuseAction-Articles&A-196.

Marin Child Care Council (2000). *Childhood emergencies: What to do.* Boulder, CO: Bull Publishing Co.

Stoll, B. H. (2000). *A to Z health and safety in the child care setting.* St. Paul, MN: Redleaf Press.

Terrass, M. (2002). Planning for disaster. Under *Keeping children safe and healthy.* http://www.earlychildhood.com/Articles/index.cfm?FuseAction=Article&A355

Vacca, J. J. (2001). Dealing with the aftermath: Helping young children with post traumatic stress disorder (PTSD). *Dimensions of Early Childhood, 29*(3), 18–24.

SUGGESTED READINGS

Demaree, M. A. (1995). Creating safe environments for children with post-traumatic stress disorder. *Dimensions of Early Childhood, 23*(3), 31–33.

Deskin, G., & Steckler, G. (1996). *When nothing makes sense: Disaster, crisis, and their effects on children.* Minneapolis, MN: Fairview.

Greenman, J. (2002). *What happened to the world? Helping children cope in turbulent times.* New York: Bright Horizons Family Solutions.

Gruenberg, A. (1998). Creative stress management: "Put your own oxygen mask on first." *Young Children, 53*(1), 38–42.

Hearron, F., & Hildebrand, V. (2003). *Management of child development centers* (5th ed.). Upper Saddle River, NJ: Merrill/Prentice Hall.

Oehlberg, P. (1996). *Making it better: Activities for children living in a stressful world.* St. Paul: MN: Redleaf Press.

Richards, T., & Bates, C. (1997). Recognizing posttraumatic stress in children. *Journal of School Health, 67(*10), 441–443.

Uhlenberg, J. M. (1996). After the alarm rings. *Young Children, 51*(2), 46–47.

Sleek, S. (1998). After the storm, children play out fears. *APA Monitor, 29*(6).

CHILDREN'S BOOKS

Cuyler, M. (2001). *Stop drop roll.* New York: Simon & Schuster.

Hines, A. G. (1984). *Maybe a band-aid with help.* New York: Dutton.

Lewis, K., & Kirk, D. (2002). *My truck is stuck.* New York: Hyperion.

Maclean, C. K. (2002). *Even firefighters hug their moms.* New York: Dutton.

Mayo, M. (2002). *Emergency!* Minneapolis, WI: Carolrhoda.

Prigger, M. S. (2002). *Aunt Minnie and the twister.* New York: Clarion.

Siomades, L. (2002). *Cuckoo can't find you.* Honesdale, PA: Boyds Mills Press.

Tekavec, H. (2002). *Storm is coming!* New York: Dial.

Chapter 5

PERSONAL SAFETY

A THERAPEUTIC APPROACH TO
CHILD ABUSE AND NEGLECT

CHILD ABUSE

We like to think most children are safe in their homes in America. Unfortunately too many children are not. They are in homes where their parents have suffered abuse in their own childhood, and now perpetuate this vicious cycle by abusing their own children. Because this unfortunate way of "raising" children may go back for generations in their families, they may not even realize that what they are doing is improper and sometimes unlawful. Children are beaten for misbehavior, threatened, yelled at, and ridiculed. Some are sexually abused. They may be the children who come to your program in an unkempt condition, with bruises or burns on their bodies, clothes that do not fit, and extremes of behavior such as exaggerated fear, excessive aggression, or withdrawal.

You as a concerned teacher or early childhood caregiver want to help such children, but may not know how to go about it. In some cases parents need to be reported to the authorities for their misconduct. In all cases parents need to be educated in proper child rearing practices. But first of all the children must be helped. This chapter takes the position that these children need healing. Thus you need to create a therapeutic environment where children can be restored to normalcy. Your classroom needs to be a caring center where abused children can feel safe and protected from further harm, and where they are allowed to express their feelings and allow themselves to be healed.

Healing Emotional Abuse

Most child abuse, whether it is physical, sexual, or mental, carries with it an emotional element on the part of the child that needs to be healed. When parents or family members scream at their children, call them names, ridicule them, or tell them how bad they are, over and over again for a prolonged period, they are abusing them emotionally. Abused children sometimes act out their emotions violently in the classroom through hitting, biting, kicking or screaming, or else they may withdraw into themselves, often clinging to a blanket or sucking their thumbs. Unless emotional abuse like this can be healed, children may carry it with them into adulthood, causing them psychological problems such as uncontrolled rage that may be expressed with fists or bullets.

Abused children need to release such pent up emotions in order for them to heal. They are often not able to do this at home or in the presence of other adults. Bowling and Rogers (2001), who help children with their emotional growth, have this to say:

> Like adults, children are also sensitive and vulnerable to hurts. The
> hurts can cloud the inherent nature of children. But in our view
> children, and adults, come with an ability to heal through natural
> physical expressions such as laughing, crying, trembling with fear,
> raging, yawning, stretching, and animated talking. (p. 79)

Rogers says she has found that staying physically close to a child having an emotional upheaval, perhaps with only a hand on a shoulder, but not trying to talk him out of crying, seems to help the most. You remember from Chapter 1 that crying is not the hurt but the process of becoming unhurt. Your silent attentive closeness to the child seems to help him more than anything when he realizes you are there as a support, not to stop him from expressing his feelings. Your hand on his shoulder tells him that you care for him. Even children who scream for you to go away will eventually accept your presence. Afterward they appear to be more relaxed, open, and content. This silent attentive closeness also works with children who withdraw. Most children in the throes of strong emotion seem to realize you accept them even when they are crying or withdrawing, and that you are standing by them, waiting for them to finish.

Then, if it seems appropriate, you can re-direct them to an activity you have set up for children to vent their frustrations harmlessly. Bowling and Rogers encourage emotionally stressed-out children to throw water baggies at targets, kick stacks of boxes, stomp on egg cartons, hit pillows, or pound their anger into clay. (p. 80) You can arrange a private area of the classroom to which children can retreat when they are upset and need to vent their feelings.

FIGURE 5.1

Strategies to Help Children Release Strong Feelings
1. Stay physically close to child having an emotional upheaval.
2. Focus your complete attention on the child.
3. Allow child to continue expressing feelings through crying, harmless hitting, screaming.
4. Do not try to talk child out of expressing the feelings.
5. Redirect child into emotion-releasing activities.

Book with a Behavior Acceptance Theme

Sometimes I'm Bombaloo (Vail, 2002)

Katie Honors tells the story of how she is really a good kid and smiles a lot and gives excellent hugs, but sometimes she is Bombaloo who shows her teeth and makes fierce noises. She uses her feet and fists instead of words. There's a lot of yelling when she's Bombaloo, and she is sent off to bed to take some time to think about it. But when she is Bombaloo she doesn't want to think about it, she wants to smash stuff. She starts throwing all of her clothes out of her drawers, but when a pair of underpants lands on her head, she laughs. And then she is Katie Honors again. It's scary being Bombaloo, but her mother knows that, and hugs her when she is herself again.

The large and lively cartoon-like illustrations make this a book children love to look at, to talk about, and to listen to again and again. Can they tell about when they are sometimes Bombaloo and what happens then?

Helping Parents of Emotionally Abused Children

What about the parents who caused such distress in the first place? Won't they continue to berate their children, keeping the cycle of children's emotional outbursts going? It is important to reach all parents with every means possible by having monthly parent newsletters in which you offer positive suggestions for children's behavior management, as well as individual parent conferences where you stress the child's accomplishments, and meetings with all the parents where you show a video such as: *Painting a Positive Picture: Proactive Behavior Management,* which shows how adults can help children manage their behavior in a nurturing and positive manner, while supporting each child's self-esteem. (National Association for the Education of Young Children, NAEYC, 2002, p. 42)

Afterward, have the parents discuss the video and compare it with behavior management techniques they have tried. Abusive parents may pick up some tips on positive behavior management from the others. To conclude the meeting, give each parent an NAEYC brochure such as *Love and Learn: Positive Guidance for Young Children,* which tells how discipline need not be punitive. Invite them to come in and talk with you about how they are getting along with their children, and what else might be helpful. You need to be as accepting of these parents, (but not of their negative behavior), as you are of their children, for their actions seem to show that they, too, are hurting. How will they ever change if no one shows them a better way to raise children? In addition, invite them to your classroom to see how positive behavior management works with the group of children.

Healing Physical Abuse

Physical abuse of a preschool child is caused by an adult inflicting or allowing the infliction of physical injury by other than accidental means. (Nunnelley & Fields, 1999, p. 76). It may be difficult for you as a teacher or child caregiver to deal with the deliberate injuring of an innocent young child, but you must take it upon yourself to confront this problem. It is the child's safety that is at stake. You may be the one who ultimately saves him or her. Just as you keep your classroom and playground as free from the danger of injuries as possible, so you must try to prevent other intentional injuries from happening to children. As Turner (2000) tells us:

> Can we keep children safe from all physical and emotional harm,
> at all times, every day, for each moment? Certainly not! But
> knowing how they are growing and paying close attention to
> each child's unique path, we can affirm that we are doing our
> best to provide safety during children's development. (p. 31)

However, you must approach the problem cautiously. Do you recognize all the signs of physical abuse? Some injuries or bruises could be caused by other factors. Children frequently fall, which may result in scrapes and bruises on knees, elbows, shins, and forehead. Other children may have had medical procedures that have left bruises.

Before you report the physical abuse of a child, check for both physical and behavior indicators. Has the child had recurring injuries, such as bruises, lacerations, welts, burns, or unexplained fractures? Are the injuries on the child's back, thighs, buttocks, face, or back of the legs? What about the child's behavior? Is she a usually happy child who has suddenly become withdrawn? Does she show fear of punishment? Of going home? Does she come from a community plagued with violence and drug abuse? (Nunnelley & Fields, p. 77)

As a teacher you do not have to prove the suspected case, but simply report your suspicions to the proper authorities such as your center director or school principal. The Child Protective Services will then be notified. If this agency decides that action should be taken, a case worker will be sent to the home to investigate. If abuse is indicated they may provide family counseling or training of some sort. In severe cases, removal of the child to a foster home may occur.

Do not feel guilty that you were the one who reported the case. You may have saved the child's life. You have stopped the physical abuse. Now it is up to you to help heal the child's inner turmoil. Developing safe feelings within a child involves helping the child feel accepted, appreciated, and cared for as discussed in Chapter 1, and especially by helping the child feel she is not to blame for being physically abused. You may already be working with this child by using some of the strategies from Figure 1.4, Strategies to Help Children Feel Accepted, but there is one more type of support you can offer a child who has been beaten down by life like this: laughter. As Mark Twain has written: "Against the assault of laughter, nothing can stand." (Twain, 1914). Turner agrees when she tells us:

> We must give back to children the fun gift of humor because
> they must deal with the harshness from the words and actions
> of others and the larger world. (p. 33)

How can you or the child laugh in the face of physical abuse? Try directing the child's attention to others who have thought they were guilty or to blame for what happened to them. Read him a funny book about it. Get him to laugh at the characters in the book. Pretend to be one of the characters yourself. Get him to laugh at you.

Books with a Not-My-Fault Theme

It Wasn't My Fault (Lester, 1985)

Things did not always go well for Murdley Gurdson in this book. He was always stumbling and bumbling around falling into wastebaskets. One day when he went for a walk in one big shoe (he couldn't remember where he left the other one), a bird laid an egg on his head! When Murdley confronted a nearby bird, she admitted it, but said it wasn't her fault because an aardvark had screamed and scared her. They confronted the aardvark who also admitted it, but said it wasn't his fault because a pigmy hippo had stepped on his tail making him scream. And so it goes as one after another animal says it wasn't my fault. But when Murdley comes to a big hopping shoe with rabbit ears sticking out, he realizes it was his fault after all for walking out of his shoe so that a rabbit got stuck in it—and two big tears roll down his face. All the animals comfort Murdley and go back to his house where they all eat scrambled eggs from the egg on top of his head.

Did your listener laugh at the funny pictures or words? If not, try reading it again and this time make the voice of each animal sound funny: gruff, whispery, shaky, deep, or squeaky. Ask your listener to be one of the animals and you be another. It's a funny story and somehow you should be able to get a laugh out of the child.

Who Sank the Boat? (Allen, 1982)

Here is a simple story about a cow, a donkey, a sheep, a pig, and a tiny little mouse who decide to go for a boat ride in the sea. Rhyming verses tell what happens when each of the animals gets into the little red boat nearly upsetting it. But who sank the boat? Finally, when they are all safely in the tiny little mouse hops aboard and you know what happens.

Child listeners can play the parts of the animals and climb into a pretend boat built of a row of chairs—and all fall out when the boat goes down. You can read as the children re-enact the story and make all the sound effects. The rest of the class can be the audience. Does anyone laugh?

Don't Make Me Laugh (Stevenson, 1999)

Here is a hilarious no-laughing book with Mr. Frimdimpny, the alligator who is in charge, making up the rules. Rule #1: Do not laugh! Rule #2: Do not even smile. Rule #3: If you laugh or smile you have to go back to the front of the book.

Your listener might want to look in the pocket mirror you provide to practice not smiling. You should stare hard at him as long as you can without cracking a smile yourself to see if he can hold a straight face. Can he do it? Hopefully not! When you both stop laughing try reading this book in which everybody breaks the rules, including—you guessed it—Mr. Frimdimpny. Go back to the front of the book!

Healing Sexual Abuse

Sexual abuse is the most difficult child safety issue of all. It is dreadful that it should happen. It is difficult for young children to prevent it. It is more difficult for young children to report it. And it is most difficult for teachers to accept what has happened and take appropriate action. Most child sexual abuse occurs in the home. Preschools and child care centers are with few exceptions safe places for young children. However, the reporting of sexual abuse often occurs in the school because abused children may feel it is safer to talk to a trusted teacher than to someone in the home where the abuse occurred. Thus teachers may be involved in all three aspects of child protection programs concerned with sexual abuse: prevention, detection, and intervention.

Prevention

The personal safety of the children in your care includes protecting them from victimization by predatory adults. You may want the children to know: who are the predatory adults, how will they approach the children, and what should the children do to prevent the abuse. All three of these aspects are very difficult for children three, four, and five years old to handle successfully. Teachers have used videos, pictures, games, and exhortations to try to alert young children to "good touches/bad touches," or "stranger-danger." Yet it is generally not strangers who abuse children. Most child sexual abuse occurs in the home, and 85% of such abuse is perpetrated by someone the child knows. (Hull, 1986, p. 18)

It is important that children do not go with strangers or do not accept rides from people they do not know, but scare tactics and bombarding children with good touches/bad touches and stranger-danger films and lessons is out of place. It may result in children who are afraid of the other adults in the building; or who run from friendly college students; or who will not let health professionals examine them. It may make teachers and child caregivers worry that entering the bathroom area with the children in their care or helping children to clean themselves may cause children to overreact and report to their parents that they were touched. (Beaty, 2004).

What is the message we want to get across to children? It should not be that there is danger in every stranger. It should not be one of "good touches" and "bad touches." How is a preschooler to distinguish between the two? With such messages we may be producing a generation of paranoid children who will keep their distance from one another as adults. Do we want to live in a society where caring, touching, and loving are perceived as threatening acts? Instead, we should encourage children to do the following:

1. Talk to a trusted adult when they feel uncomfortable.
2. Go only with a trusted adult on the street or in a car.
3. Ask a trusted adult when they are unsure of what to do.
4. Say "no" to anyone else and leave quickly.

Detection

In a few cases abuse is reported to a trusted teacher by the child. But with most preschool children it is the teacher or another staff member who discovers on her own indications that something is wrong. The child may exhibit unusual behavior. She may keep away from other children, have pain in walking, or have difficulty urinating. Teachers can talk quietly with the child if she wants to say anything, but asking leading questions or prying into home affairs is not acceptable. You need to know your program's policy for handling possible sexual abuse. You need to report your suspicions to the proper authority, usually your director or principal. Once it is decided to report the abuse to a child protective service, no one should question the child further until an agency representative is present. The abuse is traumatic enough for the child to endure. Having to repeat her story over and over only makes a bad situation worse. Instead, you need to continue your normal efforts to help the child feel good about herself, and to let her know that you are there to help her. (Nunnelley & Fields, 1999, p. 78)

You yourself may need help if you feel guilty about reporting the child. Parents may be angry, the child may be removed from the program, and even your administration may by upset with you for "rocking the boat." Keep in mind it is your concern for the child and her safety that should take precedence in your thoughts and actions. You may want to talk with someone else who has reported a case of sexual abuse for advice and counseling.

Intervention

For the agency that is handling the case, intervention means intervening in the situation by stopping the abuse and punishing the abuser. It may also mean taking the child out of the home or requiring the abuser to have counseling. For you, the teacher, intervention means helping the child to recover from the traumatic circumstances she has experienced. Spend extra time playing with the child, reading her books of her choice, or suggesting an interesting activity she might want to pursue with another child.

The child may experience post traumatic stress disorder as discussed in Chapter 4. Review Figure 4.2, Some Symptoms of Children's Post Traumatic Stress Disorder to see if the child exhibits any or many of these symptoms. The symptoms may not occur immediately because the child may have blocked out the event. Later if you notice any of these symptoms you may want to pursue one-on-one quiet activities with the child, especially if she is withdrawn. On the other hand, if she is releasing feelings of anger through hitting or throwing things, try to re-direct her into an emotion-releasing activity as mentioned in Figure 5.1, Strategies to Help Children Release Strong Feelings. Do not try to stop the child from expressing her feelings. So many children suppress the hurtful feelings of sexual abuse, and as a result carry them with them for the rest of their lives where they may reappear later in other destructive guises.

In cases of sexual abuse, some people tend to blame the victim. Young children victims often blame themselves. You must keep it uppermost in your mind that children are never to blame. They are victims of predatory adults. If you can help them release their pent-up feelings about sexual abuse, you may be saving them from a lifetime of anguish and remorse. Set up a private area in the classroom with a dollhouse, dollhouse furniture, and figures of people—families. Let the child play out her anger by hitting the people or having the people hit one another if she wants. This may sound inappropriate, but if it helps her destructive feelings to be released, and she sees that you allow it, then this may be the best you can do for her. Have a daily period where she can play out her family scenario alone, and eventually she and it may calm down.

CHILD NEGLECT

When we consider the abundance most Americans experience compared with the rest of the world, how are we to rationalize the amount of poverty that still exists, especially in the inner cities? Will poverty always be with us? Is there not something we can do to break its vicious cycle of deprivation, depression, and child neglect? Early childhood educators feel that there is. We feel that rescuing the young children of poverty through programs offering a safe and healthy environment, inviting learning activities, nutritious meals, and warm and caring teachers can help them to break out of poverty.

When an adult deprives a child of the conditions necessary for appropriate development, such as food, shelter, clothing, medical care, and maternal nurturing, it is considered neglect. Although some child neglect can occur among the affluent, it is the children of poverty who suffer the most. They often come from single parent families where the mother herself suffers from neglect or depression because of overcrowded conditions, lack of financial support, poor furnishings, poor sanitation, lack of food and clothing, unemployment, immaturity (often under 18 years), lack of knowledge about child rearing, and sometimes drug abuse.

This is not to say that all poor families are neglectful. Most are not, and some better-off families also neglect their children. When young children are allowed to run wild with no supervision and no rules or limits, they may be neglected, no matter where they are from. When children's basic needs are not met, they are considered neglected. If child neglect is not halted before children reach the age of five, even their cognitive development may be markedly impaired. (Dubowitz, Papas, Black, & Starr, 2002, p. 1100)

Healing Child Neglect

You may note that children who suffer from child neglect are often severely underweight. They may have dark circles under their eyes, be inappropriately dressed with clothing too large or too small for them, and exhibit uncleanliness as well as immature physical development. (Nunnelley & Fields, 1999, p. 76). Some may seem to be continually hungry and may eat ravenously in your program. While some neglected children act withdrawn in the classroom, others act out aggressively.

More and more child neglect these days is based on family substance abuse, especially with mothers being addicted to alcohol or drugs. What little money the family obtains goes for drugs or alcohol, not for feeding or clothing the children. The children are often left to fend for themselves. As Rice and Sanoff (1998) point out:

> One of the most compelling examples of what children live with and learn
> in an addicted family is the primary rule of the family disease: Don't Talk.
> Don't Trust. Don't Feel. Children are taught not to talk about the disease,
> ask for any help outside the family, trust anyone, and above all, feel anything.
> Just as the addict numbs over her feelings, her children learn to cope with
> their own fear, sadness, and pain by numbing themselves. The family closes
> around the disease, and the children are trapped inside. (p. 30)

If you suspect that drugs or alcohol may be the cause of the child neglect you have encountered, your program needs to focus on the difficult task of helping both child and mother with family focused interventions that encourage talking, trusting, and feeling. Therapeutic counseling where mothers learn to get in touch with their own feelings is a first step. As a teacher your principal focus will be on the child in the classroom, but your program should respond to the parents' needs.

Even though society tends to respond to any neglected children's basic needs first: i.e., food, clothing, and shelter, these children are also severely deprived of love and appreciation. Their environment is, in fact, one of little verbal or emotional interaction with adults, especially the mother. This is a significant need you and your program must address. Is this a safety issue, you may wonder? Keeping children personally safe is indeed an important safety issue. To keep neglected children safe, they must first be healed. While your program's social services may see to the food, shelter, and clothing needs of the children as well as therapeutic counseling with the parents, you and the early childhood staff must respond to neglected children's emotional needs.

How will you do it? As you may recall from Chapter 1, you yourself will need to show unconditional compassion toward a neglected child. He may be withdrawn or overly aggressive at first. This is a natural reaction for him in a new situation. But what are some of his positive aspects? Observe him closely to see. You find out that his name is Lonnie. Let him know how much you like that name. Then take him by the hand, if he will let you, and walk him slowly around the room, pointing out all of the learning centers and what goes on in them. If Lonnie shows any curiosity at all toward something in the classroom—say, the hermit crab in the science center cage, let him know how much you appreciate his interest. Would he like to find out more about hermit crabs?

Give him the little book *The Seashore* (Jeunesse, 1990) with the picture of a hermit crab on the cover and ask him to try and find any pictures of hermit crabs inside the book. When he finds the pictures read him what it says about hermit crabs living inside empty shells and having to find a bigger shell when they grow bigger. Would Lonnie like you to read him a story about a hermit crab that needs to find a bigger shell in a hurry? The book *Is This a House for Hermit Crab?* (McDonald, 1990) traces a little crab's search for a new shell and finally finding one. If any other children want to hear this story ask Lonnie if it would be all right with him to include one or two other children. Let him pick the children.

You are now helping this child develop a safe feeling within himself by feeling accepted by you and the other children as suggested in Figure 1.4 Strategies to Help Children Feel Accepted. This one small interest of Lonnie's can be extended into other areas of the classroom in the days ahead where Lonnie can paint pictures of the crab, build a block house for the crab, take a photo of the crab, tape record a story about the crab, sort a collection of seashells from smallest to largest, and finally participate in a contest to see who can find a new house that the class's hermit crab will accept.

How can you spend so much time with this one child when you have 17 other youngsters in the class? Your classroom setup and the materials in each learning center can occupy the other children. Your assistants or volunteers can circulate around the room helping the others get involved while you work with Lonnie. Eventually Lonnie will feel secure enough within himself to work and play on his own or with the others.

But you will continue to greet him by name when he comes in the morning, telling him how glad you are to see him just as you do with all the children. Neglected children are often chronically absent from school, so you may need to spend extra time encouraging him to come the next day. Can he borrow a book or toy from the "take home box" that he will need to return the next day? Your own unconditional acceptance of Lonnie may be the key that helps him recover his own feeling about himself as a worthy person, a person who deserves to be fed, clothed, sheltered, and loved.

THIS CHAPTER'S ROLE

Chapter 5, Personal Safety looks at child abuse and neglect from the standpoint of helping children to heal who have suffered from these wrongs. Emotional abuse is described with suggestions for healing this abuse, helping children release strong feelings, and helping parents of emotionally abused children. Recognizing and healing physical abuse are described along with children's books and activities that can help in the healing process. Sexual abuse, the most difficult child abuse issue, is presented, first discussing prevention and how to help children ward off predatory adults. How a teacher can detect child sexual abuse and report it to the proper authorities is considered. Finally, intervention, in which a teacher helps an abused child to heal includes the possibility of post traumatic stress disorder. Child neglect, with its roots in poverty, is examined, and helping a child to heal from neglect is described.

WHAT HAVE YOU LEARNED FROM THIS CHAPTER?

1. How can you provide a therapeutic environment in which abused children can heal?

2. What may happen with children whose emotional abuse is not healed?

3. How can you recognize an emotionally abused child?

4. How can you help an emotionally abused child to heal?

5. What can you do to help parents of emotionally abused children to change their methods of child rearing?

6. What are the signs of physical abuse of a child?

7. What should you do if you suspect that a child is being physically abused?

8. Why is it not helpful to bombard young children with films and talks about stranger-danger and good touches-bad touches?

9. What are the signs of sexual abuse in a child?

10. How can you help a child to heal from sexual abuse?

HOW CAN YOU APPLY WHAT YOU HAVE LEARNED?

1. Set up an activity in which an emotionally distressed child can vent feelings harmlessly.

2. Help a distressed child to feel accepted and appreciated by reading one of the books suggested with a not-my-fault theme.

3. Talk with a teacher who has reported child sexual abuse and find out what the procedure is in your program and what problems you might encounter.

4. Set up a dollhouse with furniture and family figures and encourage a distressed child to play out her feelings, or use one of the strategies in Figure 5.1.

5. Talk with a parent of an unruly child about how they discipline this child, and discuss alternative methods of guidance used in your program.

6. Obtain a video on abuse and neglect or behavior management and show and discuss it in a staff meeting or parent meeting.

7. Learn more about drug and alcohol abuse within families and arrange for your program to bring in a speaker, or have a health professional discuss how to help children and families in which addiction is a problem.

8. Start a card file in which you record an individual interest for each of the children in the class.

9. Bring in children's picture books on one of the topics from your card file and read a book or two to the child expressing this interest.

10. Set up extension activities based on the book reading that will help this child accept himself and become more open with his feelings.

REFERENCES

Beaty, J. J. (2004). *Skills for preschool teachers* (7th ed.). Upper Saddle River, NJ: Merrill/Prentice Hall.

Bowling, H. J., & Rogers, S. (2001). The value of healing in education. *Young Children, 56*(2), 79–81.

Dubowitz, H., Papas, M. A., Black, M. M., & Starr, R. H. (2002). Child neglect: Outcomes in high-risk urban preschoolers. *Pediatrics, 109*(6), 1100.

Hull, K. (1986). *Safe passages: A guide for teaching children personal safety.* (No city): Dawn Sign Press.

National Association for the Education of Young Children (brochure). *Love and learn: Positive guidance for young children.* Washington, D.C.: Author.

National Association for the Education of Young Children (video). *Painting a positive picture: Proactive behavior management.* Washington, D.C.: Author.

Nunnelley, J. C., & Fields, T. (1999). Anger, dismay, guilt, anxiety—The realities and roles in reporting child abuse. *Young Children, 54*(5), 74–79.

Rice, K. F., & Sanoff, M. K. (1998). Growing strong together: Helping mothers and their children affected by substance abuse. *Young Children, 53*(1), 28–33.

Turner, S. B. (2000). Caretaking of children's souls: Teaching the deep song. *Young Children, 55*(1), 31–33.

Twain, M. (1916). *The mysterious stranger.* New York: Harper.

SUGGESTED READINGS

American Academy of Pediatrics. (2002). *Caring for our children: National health and safety performance standards—Guidelines for out-of-home child care programs.* Elk Grove Village, IL: Author.

Austin, J. S. (2000). When a child discloses sexual abuse: Immediate and appropriate teacher responses. *Childhood Education, 77*(1), 2–5.

Bonner, B. L., Crow, S. M., & Logue, M. B. (1999). Fatal child neglect. In Dubowitz, H. (Ed.), *Neglected children: Research, practice and policy.* Thousand Oaks, CA: Sage Publications.

Crespi, T. D. (2002). Child sexual abuse: Offenders, disclosure, and school-based initiatives. *Adolescence, 37*(145), 151.

Ferber, J., & Koplow, L. (1996). The traumatized child in preschool. In Koplow, L. (Ed.). *Unsmiling faces: How preschools can heal.* New York: Teachers College Press.

Gowan, J. (1993). *Effects of neglect on the early development of children: Final report.* Washington, D.C.: National Clearinghouse on Child Abuse and Neglect.

Greenberg, R. (1999/2000). Substance abuse in families: Educational issues. *Childhood Education, 76*(2), 66–69.

Hearron, P. F., & Hildebrand, V. (2003). *Management of child development centers* (5th ed.). Upper Saddle River, NJ: Merrill/Prentice Hall.

Jordan, N. H. (1993). Sexual abuse programs in early childhood education: A caveat. *Young Children, 48*(6), 76–79.

CHILDREN'S BOOKS

Allen, P. (1982). *Who sank the boat?* New York: Coward-McCann.

Jeunesse, G., & Cohat, E. (1990). *The seashore.* New York: Scholastic.

Lester, H. (1985). *It wasn't my fault.* Boston: Houghton Mifflin.

McDonald, M. (1990). *Is this a house for hermit crab?* New York: Orchard.

Stevenson, J. (1999). *Don't make me laugh.* New York: Farrar, Straus, & Giroux.

Vail, R. (2002). *Sometimes I'm Bombaloo.* New York: Scholastic.

Chapter 6

TEACHING AND LEARNING
SAFE BEHAVIOR

THE ROLE OF PLAY

THE ROLE OF PLAY

Young children ages three to five learn best through play. If the play is self-directed and they are in charge, the learning is even more effective. Adults often relegate the notion of play to that of recreation, without realizing that children's play is their mode for learning to be an adult. Children cannot behave or think as an adult simply by imitating adult behaviors. They lack the means of constructing adult knowledge. (Van Hoorn, Nourot, Scales, & Alward, 2003). As teachers we sometimes forget that young children's mode of thinking is different than ours. Their means of acquiring knowledge and skills is not by listening to someone talk or by reading a book, but through play. As Van Hoorn, et al, point out:

> As educators, we must recognize that we cannot cause the child to learn.
> Our responsibility is to set the conditions for learning and development.
> We've emphasized the importance of play as one of the conditions for
> development…By supporting play in the classroom, we create a condition
> for children to learn the school content in a way that honors their
> development. (p. 326)

Some teachers still believe that "telling is teaching." But with young children it is not the teaching but the learning that counts. They learn by fooling around with things; by trying out how things works or don't work; by imagining, pretending, and imitating—that is young children's play. For real learning to take place the youngsters must be directly involved—hands on, so to speak. Even reading books to young children requires that the reader involve the listener in fun ways for the story to be meaningful.

How does learning through play apply to safety? If we want young children to learn how to be safe in this world of theirs, they can learn best through playing around with the safety rules and concepts presented in this book. It will require you as a teacher to "set the conditions," in other words, to set up the learning centers of the classroom in ways that children can teach themselves what you want them to learn through hands-on, self-directed playful activities.

How Can Children Learn Safety Through Play?

What is it you want children to learn? One way to handle the number of safety ideas presented in this text is to go through the chapters, looking especially at the figures, and extracting ideas that would be valuable for the children to learn. Then look at the classroom learning centers to see which one would be best suited to teach that particular idea. Finally, you will need to set up that learning center with activities for the children to pursue in playfully teaching themselves the particular safety concept.

114

For example, in Figure 1.6, Other-Esteem Checklist, you might decide you would like the children to learn to "take turns without a fuss" and "share toys and materials." These are definitely classroom safety issues because children who refuse to take turns or share can cause arguments and even pushing or fighting until someone gets hurt. Because there is room in the block center you decide to put in it a large cardboard packing box with windows and doors cut out, to be called "the safety house." Anyone who wants to can play in the house during the free play period.

As you probably suspected everyone wants to play, and soon there are arguments and pushing. It is time to read the picture book *This Is Our House* (Rosen, 1996). It is a story about nine children who all want to play in the cardboard box house out on the playground, but red-haired George says it isn't for girls; and then it isn't for small people; it isn't for twins; it isn't for people with glasses; and it isn't for people who try to tunnel in. But when George leaves to go to the bathroom all the children crowd in and tell George when he returns that it isn't for people with red hair. That makes George relent and say it is for all the different children. It is a house for everyone, and he is included.

Ask your children what they can do to include everyone in their house. Kyle points out there are 18 of them, not nine, and that there isn't room for 18. Megan wants to take turns, but how can they do it? Finally, they decide to make five tickets for the house which they will draw out of a hat and set the timer for 10 minutes of play before the next five children get a turn.

Safety Concepts Children Can Learn Using Small Toys from Prop Boxes

Some teachers collect toys and materials for various "play themes" in which they want children to participate. Other toys can be purchased in sets from educational supply companies. These toys can be stored in labeled cardboard "prop boxes," and brought out for children to play with in the various learning centers when that play theme is being featured. For example, here are some prop boxes containing small toys for use in the block center, sand table, or on the floor:

<u>Construction Site Set</u>
Tower Crane	Construction Workers
Trucks and Trailers	Barricades; Cones
Backhoe	Wheelbarrows
Cement Mixer	Signs; Tools

115

Firefighting Set

Fire Truck	People Figures	Aquarium Tubing
Police Car	Firefighters	for Hoses
Ambulance	Police Officers	Little Ladders
TV News Truck	Doctor; Nurse	

Rescue Team Set

Ambulance	Roll-out Bed
Male and Female Medic	Medical Case and Equipment
Rescue Dog	Young Patient Figure

School Play Set

School Building	Children	School Bus
Room Furnishings	Teacher	Child in Wheelchair
Playground Equipment	Bus Driver	

Dollhouse Set

Dollhouse
Furniture
People Figures

Traffic Safety Set

Traffic Carpet or	Traffic Signs
Interlocking Squares	Police Officer
People Figures	Cars and Trucks
Rescue Workers	Ambulance
Police Car	

For programs that cannot afford to purchase commercial toys or sets, they can collect small boxes and empty containers, and glue pictures from toy catalogs of cars, trucks, and people on their sides. Children are used to playing with anything and are quite amenable to using such homemade toys. Have the children themselves paste pictures of cars and trucks onto the sides of the boxes, and they will be even more interested in playing with them.

What safety concepts do you want the children learn? Just as you did by looking at the figures in different chapters, you can also extract other safety ideas you would like the children to begin to understand better. Then look at the classroom learning centers to see which centers would be best suited to teach these concepts:

1. What to do if the fire alarm sounds.
2. How to evacuate a building safely.
3. How to cross a street safely.
4. What to do if someone gets hurt on the playground.
5. What to do if there is an earthquake.
6. What to do if there is a tornado.
7. What to do if you are out on the playground and a thunderstorm comes.
8. What to do if you fall off the climber and hurt yourself.
9. How to ride the school bus safely to school.
10. How to go home from school safely.

Choose one of the safety concepts from the list, decide what props you need, and where the children will play to act out their scenarios. For concept #1, "what to do when the fire alarm sounds," you can tell the children at morning circle time that you will be having a safety day in the block corner, the sand table, and on the circle-time rug. Four children can play in the block corner, two at the sand table, and six on the circle-time rug by choosing the appropriate learning center necklaces during the free play period. When they are finished, they can hang their necklaces back on the hooks and someone else can take their place. The rest of the children can choose to paint at the easels, listen to tapes in the listening center, or hear one of the teachers read a book in the library center.

Put the dollhouse set out in the block center along with a prop box full of fire fighting toys. Tell the children in the block center that there is a pretend fire in the dollhouse and they should help the people who live there so they won't be injured. The children may or may not follow this scenario during their play, but they are certain to do something about a fire because of the firefighting toys. Later you can visit the block center and ask them what happened. Did the people have to evacuate the building? How did they do it safely?

In the sand table put out a construction site set and a rescue team set, along with safety goggles. Tell the children the construction workers are building a highway, but there has been an accident, and one of the workers has fallen off the crane. What can they do to help him? Let children play with the toys in any way they want. Later you can return and ask the players what happened and how they helped the people. Did they follow any of the safety rules they have been learning about?

On the circle-time rug put out traffic safety props and have the children build a busy highway with the interlocking squares, or put out a large block-play carpet with streets on it, along with a traffic safety prop box, a box of small building blocks for houses, some cars, trucks, a school bus, traffic signs, and people figures. Have the youngsters create their own neighborhood. Tell them the children who live in the houses they are building need to get to school and back safely. How can the children help them? Through play such as this children have the chance to make the abstract safety concepts you have talked about more concrete and understandable through their play with three-dimensional figures.

Safety Concepts Children Can Learn with Costumes and Hats in the Dramatic Play Center

1. There has been an explosion and fire in a nearby building. What should the people in your house do to be safe?
2. Pretend this is a playground and a boy has fallen off the climbing equipment and been injured. What should you do to help?
3. Pretend this is a school and you are getting ready to go on a field trip to the zoo. How will you get ready to go?
4. Pretend you are cooking in your house and the food in one of the pans catches on fire. What will you do?
5. Pretend you are waiting to go home from school and the mothers come one by one to pick of their children, but one child is left. What will you do?
6. You are an ambulance driver going to help people at the scene of a car accident. What will you do?
7. Pretend you are a school bus driver taking a bus full of children to school and one of the children starts running around. What will you do?
8. Pretend this is a hospital and you are a doctor or nurse taking care of the people who were hurt in the accident.
9. Pretend you are a crossing guard at a busy corner, helping children to cross the street safely, and one child runs across without looking. What will you do?
10. Pretend you are a cook in the preschool kitchen and you cut your finger accidentally with a knife. What will you do?

Children love to dress up and pretend they are someone else. The roles they play are often the ones they have seen adults enacting at home, in the school, in the community, in stores and restaurants, and on television. Be sure you provide a hat-tree full of hats and shoe racks full of shoes, as well as dress-up clothes from home hanging on hooks so that children can see what is available. Hats can be donated or purchased from school supply catalogs. Be sure to include firefighters' helmets, police hats, construction workers' hardhats, a highway patrol motorcycle helmet, crossing guard hat, bus driver, and other caps and helmets, as well as safety goggles. Plastic hats of all kinds can also be obtained from party supply stores.

Dress-up costumes can be ordered from educational supply houses such as Lakeshore Learning Materials or Constructive Playthings. Firefighter, police officer, construction worker, doctor, and nurse are some of the outfits available. Or you can put together a large prop box for a doctor or nurse containing Band-Aids, bandages, cotton balls, plastic bottles, plastic thermometer, stethoscope, tongue depressors, and a medical bag. A prop box for a firefighter can contain a firefighter's helmet, old vacuum cleaner hose, toy hatchet, bucket, sponges, and boots. Once again you should talk to the children after the dramatic play scenario is finished, asking what they did and what safety rules they followed.

Safety Concepts Children Can Learn with Puppets, Character Dolls, or Stuffed Animals

1. One of your puppets has been in a car accident and is very frightened. Talk with the puppet about it and see if you can get her to calm down and stop crying.
2. This puppet is afraid of thunder and hides when he hears it. What can you do to help him overcome his fear?
3. This puppet fell off the outdoor climber and is crying because she is hurt. How can you help her?
4. These two puppets are arguing over who gets to ride on the scooter. How can you help them?
5. This puppet wants to get across a busy street but doesn't know how to do it. How can you help?
6. This puppet is Aunt Minnie from the book *Aunt Minnie and the Twister* (Prigger, 2002). She sees another tornado coming. What should she do about all the children?
7. This character doll is brother David from the book *Oonga Boonga* (Wishinsky, 1998). He was the only one who could stop Baby Louise from crying by saying "oonga boonga." She's crying again. What should he do?
8. This little duck is Chucky Ducky from the book *Earthquack!* (Palatini, 2002). She told everyone that the earth was quaking. Now she feels a rumbling and is telling everyone a volcano is erupting. What can you do?
9. This cat is Francis from the book *Francis the Scaredy Cat.* (Boxall, 2002). He is afraid of the noise he hears in the closet. What can you do?

10. This character doll is Suki from the book *Will You Come Back for Me?* (Tompert, 1988). She is still afraid her mother will not come back and pick her up when school is finished. What can you do to help her?

To introduce safety concepts children can learn with puppets, character dolls, or stuffed animals you will need to play with one or two children at a time with the puppets or dolls. Choose one of the above scenarios, put a puppet on your hand and invite a child to take another puppet. Then act out the little scene having your puppet talk to the child's puppet telling what is wrong and asking what your puppet should do. Ask another child to join you and replay the scene adding new information along the same line and asking the new puppet what to do.

If the puppets or dolls are book characters, be sure to read children the book first and then bring out the puppets. If you do not have any of the books mentioned, read any book with characters that the children like and afterwards tell them the puppets are these characters. Make up a safety scenario of your own for the puppets to act out. It does not have to follow the book story line. The idea is for children to apply what they are learning about safety to everyday situations with puppets or dolls as characters.

Safety Concepts Children Can Learn Through
Teacher-Led Follow-the-Leader Games

1. Having a fire drill
2. Going for a safety walk in the classroom
3. Going for a safety walk on the playground
4. Going for a safety walk in the bathroom
5. Going for a safety walk across a busy street
6. Going in the bus on a field trip
7. Getting on a bus and coming to school
8. Going to school in mother's car
9. Walking down the street to the park
10. Going for a weather emergency walk

Teachers can enter the fun-and-games of safety learning activities whenever they feel the need. Sometimes teachers notice that children are not following the proper procedures in their pretend safety scenarios. Instead of correcting the children, it is more effective to enter the play as a character who shows the others what to do. Some teachers prefer to remind children of how to practice safety in different locations by having a follow-the-leader pretend walk in the room with the teacher leading. Such walks should be fun learning games based on the familiar pretend game "We're Going on a Bear Hunt."

The 10 games listed can be carried out in classroom in two different ways. Children can line up and actually follow the teacher round and round the classroom, copying her actions, and repeating her words and sounds. Or the children can stand in a circle in the classroom and repeat the teacher's actions and words while standing in place as in a fingerplay.

To get the children started play "We're Going on a Bear Hunt" with them standing in a circle and repeating your words and motions. You may want to read the book *We're Going on a Bear Hunt* (Rosen and Oxenbury, 1989) if the children are not familiar with the routine. After they have performed the Bear Hunt actions a few times, change the game to one of the safety concepts mentioned above. For example, "We're having a fire drill." Here is how one teacher converted the Bear Hunt words to this game:

We're having a fire drill,	(Motion for everyone to come)
We're having a fire drill,	(Repeat)
We're having a fire drill	(Repeat)
But we're not scared	(Hands on hips; shake head)
The alarm's going EEEEEEEE	(Hands over ears)
The alarm's going EEEEEEEE	(Repeat)
The alarm's going EEEEEEEE	(Repeat)
But we're not scared.	(Hands on hips, shake head)
We have to line up quickly,	(Run rapidly in place)
We have to line up quickly,	(Repeat)
We have to line up quickly,	(Repeat)
But we're not scared.	(Hands on hips, shake head)
We're marching down the hall,	(March in place)
We're marching down the hall,	(Repeat)
We're marching down the hall,	(Repeat)
But we're not scared.	(Hands on hips, shake head)
Oh, no! The door's locked!	
We have to go back again,	(Turn around in place)
We have to go back again,	(Repeat)
We have to go back again,	(Repeat)
But we're not scared.	(Hands on hips, shake head)
Oh, no! There's smoke in the hall!	
We can't go over it,	(Arms over head)
We can't go through it,	(Make swimming motion)
We have to go under it,	(Get down on floor)
But we're not scared.	(Raise up head and shake it)
Scramble, scramble,	(Crawl in place)
Scruffle, scruffle,	(Repeat)

121

Hold your nose!	(Hold nose)
But we're not scared.	(Stand up and shake head)
Now we're going downstairs,	(Take big steps)
Now we're going downstairs,	(Repeat)
Now we're going downstairs,	(Repeat)
Hold on tight!	(Put arm out; hold railing)
Now we're going outside,	(Pull open door)
Now we're going outside,	(Repeat)
Now we're going outside,	(Repeat)
But we're not scared.	(Hands on hips, shake head)
Oh, no! It's raining!	
We can't go over it,	(Duck head)
We can't go under it,	(Repeat)
We have to go through it,	(Repeat)
But we're not scared.	(Hands on hips, shake head)
Hurray, we made it safely,	(Hands over head, cheering)
Hurray, we made it safely,	(Repeat)
Hurray, we made it safely,	(Repeat)
AND WE WEREN'T SCARED!	(All flop down on floor)

Children can't wait to "all flop down" at the end of this game. They usually get up laughing and giggling and want to "do it again, teacher." Is this silly activity any way to teach something as serious as a fire drill, you may wonder? Then you remember that young children learn through playful experiences. Do you also remember that "laughter stimulates the body's production of endorphins, thereby diminishing stress and even pain"? (Sylwester, 1995) When children have played through a scary scenario they are more likely not to panic when the real thing happens.

Any of the safety concepts listed can be made into bear-hunt follow-the-leader games like this. Use your imagination to think of things that will interfere within the various safety walks you might take, and what funny words and motions you and the children can make to overcome such blockades. Whether you stand in a circle or walk around in a circle children love to repeat these follow-the-leader safety games. For the school bus or field trip bus activity, you can set up chairs one behind the other and be the driver of the bus while children sit in the bus seats and repeat the verse and motions you have made up. Then it is their turn to be the drivers.

Other Teacher-Led Safety Activities

Getting children's attention quickly

> Turn off the overhead light. Say loudly and clap: "One, two, three! Freeze like me!" Raise one hand above your head. The children must stop what they are doing and raise one hand above their heads. Then you can make an announcement; tell children what they must do when you turn on the lights; or give some kind of safety direction.

Filling the emergency duffel bag

> Have an empty duffel bag in front of you at circle time. Ask "Who can find something in the room we should take with us in our emergency duffel bag when there is a fire drill?" Have one child at a time find something and put it in the bag. It can be a pretend item or a real one. Ask the child what it is and ask who knows why we should take it in our bag.

Having children identify moods and emotions

> Obtain a poster pack of Moods and Emotions pictures showing faces of 20 children exhibiting all kinds of emotions from Lakeshore Learning Materials. At circle time have one child at a time choose a picture and hold it up for the others to see. Who can tell what the child in the picture feels like? What do you think might have made him or her feel like that?

Use a safety video with puppets

> Three short 10-minute safety videos featuring the popular Schiffely Puppets are available from Demco Kids and Things. Show each video on different days in the Listening Center for a small group at a time until everyone has seen it. Then give children several puppets to make up a pretend scenario about these topics:
> *The Adventures of Safety Frog: Seat Belts Are for Kids Too*
> *The Adventures of Safety Frog: Tornado Safety*
> *The Adventures of Safety Frog: Fire Safety*

THIS CHAPTER'S ROLE

Safety in the preschool is serious business. We understand this as we become more aware every passing day of the perils confronting all of us. We also understand that as teachers of preschool children we need to take seriously our role in the education and protection of these youngsters. Nevertheless, the strategies we choose to use in this endeavor must tap into the child's own world of play. As Van Hoorn, et al, point out: "Because children make of the world what they wish, we say that children are bound by play, where work and practice are tied to pretense, fantasy, and imitation." (p. 320)

Only when we tap into this play mode of young children can we accomplish our goals of helping children learn what they must do to be safe in a way that strengthens their inner core so that they may face the world with confidence, not fear.

WHAT HAVE YOU LEARNED FROM THIS CHAPTER?

1. Why is play so important in young children's learning?

2. How can you help children learn safety concepts through play?

3. What safety concepts should you help children learn?

4. How can you use small toys to help children learn safety?

5. How can children learn safety in the dramatic play center?

6. How can you use puppets to help children learn safety concepts?

7. How can teachers help children to learn safety concepts through a follow-the-leader game?

8. What is one way to get children's immediate attention?

9. How can children learn what other children feel like?

10. How can you use videos to help children learn safety concepts?

HOW CAN YOU APPLY WHAT YOU HAVE LEARNED?

1. What evidence have you seen that children actually learn through play?

2. How would you set up a learning center for children to teach themselves about taking turns without a fuss or sharing toys and materials?

3. Make a collection of small toys for a safety theme prop box that will help children learn a safety concept. Describe how you will use it and what you would expect children to learn.

4. Help children make a set of toys to be used to teach safety in a learning center and put them to use.

5. Choose a safety concept such as a particular weather emergency and tell how you would set up a learning center with toys to help children learn what to do.

6. How would you set up the dramatic play center for children to be involved in a play scenario about being an ambulance driver and going to help people in a car accident?

7. How would you set up the dramatic play center for children to pretend they are cooks in the preschool kitchen and have cut their fingers and need help.

8. Use a puppet who is afraid of thunder and hides in an activity with children. What can the children think of to do to help him?

9. Read one of the children's books mentioned in this text to a group of children and pretend a puppet is one of the characters. Have her ask the children what they would have done if things in the book had happened to them.

10. Make up a follow-the-leader safety game and play it with the children. How do they respond? What do you think they learned?

REFERENCES

Sylwester, R. (1995). *A celebration of neurons: An educator's guide to the human brain.* Alexandria, VA: Association for Supervision and Curriculum Development.

Van Hoorn, J, Nourot, P. M., Scales, B., & Alward, K. R. (2003). *Play at the center of the curriculum* (3rd ed.). Upper Saddle River, NJ: Merrill/Prentice Hall.

SUGGESTED READINGS

Brokering, L. (1989). *Resources for dramatic play.* Carthage, IL: Fearon Teacher Aids.

Garmezy, N., Masters, A. S., & Tellegsan, N. (1984). The study of stress and competence in children. *Child Development, 55*(1), 97–111.

Krall, C. M., & Jalongo, M. R. (1998/99). Creating a caring community in classrooms: Advice from an intervention specialist. *Childhood Education, 75*(2), 83–89.

Novick, R. (1998). The comfort corner: Fostering resiliency and emotional intelligence. *Childhood Education,* (Summer), 200–204.

Novick, R. (2002). Nurturing emotional literacy: Learning to read the heart. *Young Children, 57*(3), 84–89.

CHILDREN'S BOOKS

Boxall, E. (2002). *Francis the scaredy cat.* Cambridge, MA: Candlewick Press.

Palatini, M. (2002). *Earthquack!* New York: Simon & Schuster.

Rosen, M. (1996). *This is our house.* Cambridge, MA: Candlewick Press.

Prigger, M. S. (2002). *Aunt Minnie and the twister.* New York: Clarion.

Rosen, M., & Oxenbury, H. (1989). *We're going on a bear hunt.* New York: Margaret K. McElderry Books.

Tompert, A. (1988). *Will you come back for me?* Morton Grove, IL: Whitman.

Wishinsky, F. (1998). *Oonga boonga.* New York: Dutton.

EDUCATIONAL SUPPLY COMPANIES

Constructive Playthings
13201 Arrington Rd.
Grandview, MO 64030
1-800-448-4115

Demco Kids & Things
P.O. Box 7488
Madison, WI 53707
1-800-356-1200

Lakeshore Learning Materials
2695 E. Dominguez St.
Carson, CA 90810
1-800-421-5354